PENGUIN CLASSICS

PHÈDRE

JEAN RACINE was born in 1639 at La Ferté Milon, sixty miles
east of Paris. Orphaned at an early age, he was educated at the
Little Schools of Port Royal and the pro-Jansenist College of
Beauvais. He soon reacted against his austere mentors and by
1660 he had begun to write for the theatre and had been
introduced to the court of Louis XIV. In 1677, when he had
ten plays to his credit and was high in favour with both the
court and the public, he abandoned the theatre, which was
regarded as far from respectable by the Church, and joined the
Establishment as Royal Historiographer. It was only after a
silence of twelve years that he wrote his last two plays (both on
religious subjects), *Esther* and *Athaliah*. He died in 1699.

MARGARET RAWLINGS, in private life Lady Barlow, is a
distinguished English actress who is also a French scholar.
She was born in Japan and educated at Oxford High School
for Girls and Lady Margaret Hall, Oxford. Miss Rawlings
has been a professional actress since 1927 and has played
many Shakespearean and Shavian heroines in addition to
innumerable other important roles. In 1957 Campbell Allen
produced in London a theatre-in-the-round version of *Phèdre*,
and Miss Rawlings' performance in the title role was widely
acclaimed by the critics.

PHÈDRE

PHÈDRE

by
JEAN RACINE

translated by
MARGARET RAWLINGS

O doux et grand Racine
Anatole France

PENGUIN BOOKS

PENGUIN BOOKS
Published by the Penguin Group
Penguin Books USA Inc.,
375 Hudson Street, New York, New York 10014, U.S.A.
Penguin Books Ltd, 27 Wrights Lane,
London W8 5TZ, England
Penguin Books Australia Ltd, Ringwood,
Victoria, Australia
Penguin Books Canada Ltd, 10 Alcorn Avenue
Toronto, Ontario, Canada M4V 3B2
Penguin Books (N.Z.) Ltd, 182–190 Wairau Road,
Auckland 10, New Zealand

Penguin Books Ltd, Registered Offices:
Harmondsworth, Middlesex, England

First published in the United States of America by E. P. Dutton 1962
Published in Penguin Books 1991

3 5 7 9 10 8 6 4

ISBN 0 14 04.4591 9

Printed in the United States of America

CONTENTS

Translation is always a treason, and, as a Ming author observes, can at its best be only the reverse side of a brocade,—all the threads are there, but not the subtlety of colour or design.

Okakura Kakuzo: THE BOOK OF TEA

FOREWORD

I know that it is not possible to translate the incomparable verse of Jean Racine. But I think it a pity that one of the five greatest plays in the world should be lost to the English-speaking theatre, and to students, for want of a translation. Shakespeare cannot really be translated either. But generations of French children have known the plots, the characters, the arguments and philosophies of his plays, whereas only a few English have ever heard of the plays of Racine. French children and actors know that there is a great poet and dramatist called Shakespeare; his plays are often performed in French. But English children and actors hardly know that Racine exists. His plays are not performed in English. Most of all I think it is a pity for actresses to lose the chance of playing one of the few great parts there are for an actress. One of the reasons why there are great actors in the English drama, and great actresses in the French, is that Shakespeare was writing for men and boys, while Racine was writing for women.

If an English poet were to translate *Phèdre*, we might have a wonderful play. It would be *Phèdre*—or *Phaedra*—after Racine, after Euripides, but it would not be a *translation* of Racine's *Phèdre*. Mine is. This version is exact to its original in meaning and in feeling. It is speakable and actable. There have had to be sacrifices of course. When driven to desperation because of the necessity to lose some subtlety of the French, I have been guided by how the line will sound when spoken by the actor. There are many lines here, I am only too well aware, that can be ridiculed by a scholar reading them with silent contempt, but which he would be surprised to find do not offend the ear, and which even sound quite effective when spoken aloud. Racine was writing for actors. I began this translation during rehearsals.

When, in 1957, Stephen Joseph invited me to play Phèdre in English, I did not say: Where? With whom? For how long? or For how much? I just said: Yes, at once; one of my life's two great ambitions being to play Phèdre. It turned out to be for two special

9

Sunday performances in Theatre-in-the-Round, for which he adapted the Mahatma Gandhi Hall, Fitzroy Square, and later for three weeks, followed by a tour. I soon realized why the play, or for that matter the whole wonderful drama of Racine, is not done in English. There is no actable translation. The least horrible was the version we used, made by Robert Bruce Boswell and published in Bohn's Classic Library in 1890. But its language was Victorian, and the actors and actresses made many faces at the first reading. He was, after all, only writing for scholars to read, not to act. The first laugh at rehearsal was on Theramenes' line:

> *You have been seldom seen with wild delight*
> *Urging the rapid car along the Strand!*

which conjured up in all our minds the picture of a young man in a sports car in a traffic block somewhere near the Savoy. Racine's line is:

> *On vous voit moins souvent, orgueilleux et sauvage,*
> *Tantôt faire voler un char sur le rivage . . .*

So I changed the line to:

> *You are less often seen, so proud and wild,*
> *Making a chariot fly along the shore . . .*

The word *char* is *chariot* in English. But fashions change. In 1880 chariot meant a small light carriage, usually drawn by a high-stepping pony, so Mr. Boswell avoided the word; and the word *car* did not yet exclusively mean *motor-car*, so he employed it. Now films like *Ben Hur* have once more accustomed us to the word *chariot* in its Greek sense, so it was easy to go back to a literal translation of the French. Fired by this apparently effortless improvement upon Mr. Boswell, I faced the next laugh—a ribald one this time, on the line:

> *Phaedra reaps little glory from a lover*
> *So lavish of his size . . .*

at least that is what we *heard*. It turned out to be *soupirs*—sighs! But no audience would have understood it any more than we did, so that had to be changed. Then Mr. Boswell's Hippolytus says to Aricia that he gives way to her *juster claims*. But this sounds like *just acclaims* and makes nonsense. So I made him say *claims more just*. The word *just*, meaning right and fair, causes us problems unknown to Mr. Boswell. Phaedra runs on in Act IV Scene IV saying: *My lord, I come to you filled with just dread*. It is hard not to get a laugh on this, because of the American intonation present in it. I had to change it to: My Lord, I hasten to you filled with dread. Next I found that Mr. Boswell omitted the name Erectheus in Aricia's speech in Act II Scene I, so making it almost impossible for the actress to make her meaning clear. He also, by accident or design, omitted the beautiful line:

> *Et mes coursiers oisifs ont oublié ma voix*

which I rendered as:

> *My lazy stallions have forgot my voice.*

I disliked:

> *. . . When comes to riper age*
> *Reason approved what Nature had implanted.*

for:

> *Dans un âge plus mûr moi-même parvenu,*
> *Je me suis applaudi quand je me suis connu.*

and felt that the actor could get nearer to Racine's meaning with:

> *. . . when*
> *I grew to riper years and knew myself,*
> *I praised myself the self I came to know.*

This grew. Every day someone came up to me at rehearsal and said: You've made your part better—could you do this bit for me? We groped, we argued, we patted out: *Shall I compare thee . . .* to make sure that all our syllables and stresses were right and speakable, and gradually, got most of the Victorian horrors out of our script. *Marâtre* is a good wide strong sound of only two syllables, or three when required, whereas *stepmother* is almost impossible to get into a blank verse line. I was determined to do so, and, after a struggle, managed to remove all Mr. Boswell's *stepdames* from the script.

Sometimes Racine repeats a word several times in a couple of lines.

Of course he does it on purpose. But Mr. Boswell and others, not being actors, did not think it mattered. Phèdre said: *C'est moi, Prince, c'est moi, dont l'utile secours . . .* Boswell makes her say: *And I, it would have been whose timely aid.* I think it better for her to say: *And I, it would have been, Prince, I whose aid. . . .* No actress would disagree with me.

Aricia says:

> *Mes yeux alors, mes yeux n'avaient pas vu son fils.*
> *Non que par les yeux seuls . . .*

Three eyes in two lines! Mr. Boswell did not think they mattered. From the actress's point of view they do; so I make her say:

> *But then my eyes, my eyes had never yet*
> *Beheld his son. Not that my eyes alone . . .*

After a week or two I had to give up rewriting. There is a limit to the new lines that can be learned just before a first night. But afterwards I could not help going on with the work. I rewrote the whole thing, direct from Racine. Mr. Boswell's text, of which nothing now remains except three or four lines I find too good to lose, was —apart from stepdames—sprinkled with 'tises, e'ens, o'ers, scarces, fain would I's, and ersts. I have got rid of all of them. Freed from the pruderies that muffled poor Mr. Boswell in 1890, I like to believe that this text is nearer in plain English to Racine's meaning. While avoiding old-fashioned idioms, I have not consciously tried to make this version modern. After all, we act the play in costume. But I have made Œnone and Panope and Theramenes and Ismene a trifle more colloquial in their speech than their more regal masters and mistresses.

Since finishing this work I have read several other translations of *Phèdre*. All take what I think are great liberties. There is an anonymous one in the British Museum dated 1776, in verse, but in no metre recognizable by me (some speeches in very long, and some in very short lines), in which the author completely changes the last couplet.

> *Que malgré les complots d'une injuste famille*
> *Son amante aujourd'hui me tienne lieu de fille.*

into:

12

with no word of Aricia becoming Theseus' daughter from today, which has always struck me as being such a promising end to the tragedy. I envisage Aricia and Theseus consoling each other. It would just suit Theseus.

This translator was also not happy about the wonderful: *Vénus toute entière* . . . and had buried it so deep in about four lines of verse that I was hard put to find it, and dramatically it could have no effect whatever.

In the cast list I have described Theramenes, not as tutor to Hippolytus, but as tutor and friend to Hippolytus, because I think the relationship is much more that of Horatio to Hamlet than usually appears. In the productions I have seen, everyone has been played far too old, and Theramenes has obviously been chosen in order to understudy Theseus. The play must have been far more exciting in Racine's own time, or when Rachel played Phèdre at the age of twenty-two, and Bernhardt at twenty-eight. Because it takes trained speakers to be able to sing the tirades, those wonderful cascades of words which from time to time gush forth with effortless but lively accuracy of diction, Phèdre and Thésée are often so lacking in youth that in the eyes of anyone young in the audience the whole plot is indecent or at least laughably unlikely. I long to see the play done with a Phaedra of not over thirty-five, a Theseus of not over forty-five, and a Hippolytus of not under twenty-five. Theramenes is a little older than Hippolytus, indeed the same age as Phaedra or a little younger. Then it would be easier to believe in a story which can be true today. What we forget is how young people died of old age in those days.

When I was twenty I thought that love, in the amorous and jealousy-provoking sense, must certainly be all over by the time anyone was thirty. That an actress of fifty, sixty, or even seventy—however good an actress—should parade a guilty passion for her stepson—played by a boy—is always to make nonsense of the play, at least in the eyes of the young. And it is because I care about the young audience that I have made this translation. If Phaedra is not a day over thirty-five, married to a handsome forty-five much away on business (including helping a friend to steal a neighbouring dictator's wife), and if her stepson is about five to—at the most—ten years younger than herself, there is no difficulty whatever for an audience to get caught up in excitement and sympathy with her tragedy. The tragedy indeed exists on two planes. It is great because, as Racine explains in his preface, her moral sense is so strong that her conflict is between her passion and her duty, between her physical and her spiritual self, and is raised by her invocation of the Gods— her ancestor the Sun; her father Minos—to a spiritual level. I have seen this wonderfully done. But don't let anyone be deceived by the high-sounding curse put upon Phaedra by Venus, or, as in the original play by Euripides, put upon Hippolytus by an outraged Venus because he scorned the love of women. It was love: just violent sexual passion, and if the actress is too old for a young audience to believe in it—then it's just too bad—they have not seen the play.

The insuperable difficulty of the translator is that those glorious Alexandrines have two syllables more in each line than an English line of blank verse, and that all but one of the proper names in French are a syllable shorter than in English. I think one must use the anglicized Greek pronunciations of names because they are already familiar to us and also because some sounds are comic to an English ear. Hippolytus sounds decent, but however Hippolyte looks in print, it sounds to us like Eepoleet, and Theseus sounds better than Tayzay. So, alas, Phèdre has to be sacrificed to Phaedra, which is not, and never can sound, as beautiful, though, if the first syllable is pronounced *fed* rather than *feed* the name is nearer to the sound of the French.

I have followed the French method of placing at the head of each scene the names of those present on the stage. This makes it un- necessary to use any stage directions. An actor whose name heads a scene has entered; and one whose name is not there, but was in the previous scene, must have left the stage. But since this is unusual to English producers, and since I hope my translation will be useful to schools and repertories, I have added the direction: Exit, after Phaedra's last speech in Act IV, which is immediately followed by Œnone's last couplet and her exit. The curtain comes down on those two exits, separated only by Œnone's last words.

I have taken one liberty. In Act II Scene I, Ismène calls Theseus *cet époux infidèle*, which implies more than *this unfaithful husband*. But Chaucer called him the *great untrouthe of love*, so I have dared to use this celebrated phrase.

I use Thee and Thou only when characters address themselves to Gods. Otherwise the more easily understandable You. The distinction in formality or in the abandonment of formality, implied in French when a character changes from vous to tu, I have been obliged to lose, as has every translator before me, and will every translator after me.

It is, I know, both dangerous and presumptuous to allow my translation to be printed face to face with the original, which is to me *one entire and perfect chrysolite*. But I have been persuaded by three people whose judgment I trust, that this will make it of more use to more people.

The most difficult bit of all the translation was Phaedra's soliloquy in Act IV Scene V. Theseus goes, leaving Phaedra and the audience with the shock of her realization that Hippolytus was not insensible to love; that, in fact, *he loved another*. Her words are: *He is gone,* followed by ten lines (eleven in English) of explanation of why she had just run thither to exonerate him. I would like to cut those lines (which include exclamations like: What thunderbolt! What fatal news! which one would prefer to avoid) and, after a ghastly, deadly pause, during which the audience does not know what she will do—an almost unbearable suspense—to say the line: *Hippolytus can feel, but not for me.* From an actress's point of view it is infinitely more effective. I took the liberty of doing this in performance and always would. It is my only criticism of Racine's Phèdre. But if my saying that I believe this one short passage to be dramatically superfluous, should lead anyone to cut other passages which they might find difficult, I should regard myself as a criminal. Every word, in its order, and every line and Scene and Act, in their order, are irreplaceable in this unique dramatic poem.

Finally there is Phaedra's last speech. She is paralysed with poison. It is the same death as Cleopatra's except that the actress is standing instead of sitting on a throne. Boswell's, and all other translations I have seen, make her last words: *that they defiled,* or *which they have defiled.*

> *Death, from mine eyes, veiling the light of Heav'n*
> *Restores its purity that they defiled.* (Boswell)

But Racine's Phèdre says:

> *Et la mort, à mes yeux dérobant la clarté,*
> *Rend au jour, qu'ils souillaient, toute sa pureté.*

Her last breath is on the upward note of *toute sa pureté*, not on the downward one of: *that they defiled*. At rehearsals I tried again and again and found I could not die on that downward meaning. I found that Phaedra needs the reason for the great effort to raise an almost paralysed hand to indicate the purity about to be restored to daylight by her death. She needs it because, as the feeble hand makes its last upward gesture on the words—*all its purity*—so the strain upon that heart (now filled with icy cold by the poison brought to Athens by Medea) can be just too much for it: the thread snaps: life goes out, and she can make a spectacular fall. So, although the penultimate line is not good, and I cannot make it better, I have forced the English Phaedra to end with the very same words as the true, the original, the French Phèdre.

This attempt is dedicated to all future Phaedras with love from this one.

June 12th, 1960.   MARGARET RAWLINGS

THESEUS, king of Athens and Trozene . . *Michael Aldridge*

PHAEDRA, his wife, daughter of Minos and Pasiphaë
Margaret Rawlings

HIPPOLYTUS, son of Theseus, stepson to Phaedra . *Keith Baxter*

ARICIA, princess of Athenian blood-royal . . *Ann Sears*

ŒNONE, nurse and companion to Phaedra . *Helena Pickard*

THERAMENES, tutor to Hippolytus . . *Gerald Harper*

ISMENE, companion to Aricia . . . . *Enid Lorimer*

PANOPE, lady in waiting . . . . *Cynthia Taylor*

Produced by CAMPBELL ALLEN

PRÉFACE

Voici encore une tragédie dont le sujet est pris d'Euripide. Quoique j'aie suivi une route un peu différente de celle de cet auteur pour la conduite de l'action, je n'ai pas laissé d'enrichir ma pièce de tout ce qui m'a paru le plus éclatant dans la sienne. Quand je ne lui devrais que la seule idée du caractère de Phèdre, je pourrais dire que je lui dois ce que j'ai peut-être mis de plus raisonnable sur le théâtre. Je ne suis point étonné que ce caractère ait eu un succès si heureux du temps d'Euripide, et qu'il ait encore si bien réussi dans notre siècle, puisqu'il a toutes les qualités qu'Aristote demande dans le héros de la tragédie, et qui sont propres à exciter la compassion et la terreur. En effet, Phèdre n'est ni tout à fait coupable, ni tout à fait innocente; elle est engagée, par sa destinée et par la colère des Dieux, dans une passion illégitime, dont elle a horreur toute la première. Elle fait tous ses efforts pour la surmonter, elle aime mieux se laisser mourir que de la déclarer à personne; et lorsqu'elle est forcée de la découvrir, elle en parle avec une confusion qui fait bien voir que son crime est plutôt une punition des Dieux qu'un mouvement de sa volonté.

J'ai même pris soin de la rendre un peu moins odieuse qu'elle n'est dans les tragédies des anciens, où elle se résout d'elle-même à accuser Hippolyte. J'ai cru que la calomnie avait quelque chose de trop bas et de trop noir pour la mettre dans la bouche d'une Princesse, qui a d'ailleurs des sentiments si nobles et si vertueux. Cette bassesse m'a paru plus convenable à une nourrice qui pouvait avoir des inclinations plus serviles, et qui néanmoins n'entreprend cette fausse accusation que pour sauver la vie et l'honneur de sa maîtresse. Phèdre n'y donne les mains que parce qu'elle est dans une agitation d'esprit qui la met hors d'elle-même; et elle vient un moment après dans le dessein de justifier l'innocence et de déclarer la vérité.

Hippolyte est accusé, dans Euripide et dans Sénèque, d'avoir en effet violé sa belle-mère: *vim corpus tulit*. Mais il n'est ici accusé que d'en avoir eu dessein. J'ai voulu épargner à Thésée une confusion qui l'aurait pu rendre moins agréable aux spectateurs.

18

PREFACE

(Jean Racine 1677)

Here is another tragedy whose subject is derived from Euripides. Although I have taken, for the conduct of the action, a path a little different from the one chosen by this author, I have not neglected to enrich my play with everything I judged most dazzling in his. Even if my debt to him were only for the mere idea of the character of Phaedra I could say that I owe to him perhaps the most lively portrait I have put upon the stage. I am not surprised that this character should have had so happy a success in the time of Euripides, and that it should also have been so successful in our century, because it has all the qualities demanded by Aristotle of the central figure of a tragedy, and which are bound to excite compassion and terror. In fact, Phaedra is neither entirely guilty nor entirely innocent: she finds herself, by her destiny and by the anger of the Gods, engaged in an illicit passion of which she is the first to feel horrified. She tries with all her might to conquer it, she prefers to die rather than to declare it to anyone; and when at last she is driven to reveal it, she speaks of it with a shame which makes only too clear that her crime is rather a punishment inflicted on her by the Gods than an impulse of her own will.

I have even taken the trouble to make her a little less hateful than she is in the ancient versions of this tragedy, in which she herself resolves to accuse Hippolytus. I judged that calumny had about it something too base and too black to be put into the mouth of a Princess who for most of the time is only noble and virtuous. This depravity seemed to me more appropriate to the character of a nurse, whose inclinations might be supposed to be more servile, but who, nevertheless, only takes upon herself the responsibility for this false accusation in order to save the life and honour of her mistress. Phaedra only agrees to this because she is in an agitation of spirit so extreme as to be beside herself, and indeed, only a moment afterwards, she runs on to the scene with the intention of vindicating innocence and declaring the truth.

Pour ce qui est du personnage d'Hippolyte, j'avais remarqué dans les anciens qu'on reprochait à Euripide de l'avoir représenté comme un Philosophe exempt de toute imperfection; ce qui faisait que la mort de ce jeune Prince causait beaucoup plus d'indignation que de pitié. J'ai cru lui devoir donner quelque faiblesse qui le rendrait un peu coupable envers son père, sans pourtant lui rien ôter de cette grandeur d'âme avec laquelle il épargne l'honneur de Phèdre, et se laisse opprimer sans l'accuser. J'appelle faiblesse la passion qu'il ressent malgré lui pour Aricie, qui est la fille et la sœur des ennemis mortels de son père.

Cette Aricie n'est point un personnage de mon invention. Virgile dit qu'Hippolyte l'épousa, et en eut un fils, après qu'Esculape l'eut ressuscité. Et j'ai lu encore dans quelques Auteurs qu'Hippolyte avait épousé et emmené en Italie une jeune Athénienne de grande naissance, qui s'appelait Aricie, et qui avait donné son nom à une petite ville d'Italie.

Je rapporte ces autorités, parce que je me suis très scrupuleusement attaché à suivre la Fable. J'ai même suivi l'histoire de Thésée, telle qu'elle est dans Plutarque.

C'est dans cet Historien que j'ai trouvé que ce qui avait donné occasion de croire que Thésée fut descendu dans les enfers pour enlever Proserpine, était un voyage que ce Prince avait fait en Épire vers la source de l'Achéron, chez un Roi dont Pirithoüs voulait emmener la femme, et qui arrêta Thésée prisonnier, après avoir fait mourir Pirithoüs. Ainsi j'ai tâché de conserver la vraisemblance de l'Histoire, sans rien perdre des ornements de la Fable, qui fournit extrêmement à la Poésie. Et le bruit de la mort de Thésée, fondée sur ce voyage fabuleux, donne lieu à Phèdre de faire une déclaration d'amour qui devient une des principales causes de son malheur, et qu'elle n'aurait jamais osé faire tant qu'elle aurait cru que son mari était vivant.

Au reste, je n'ose encore assurer que cette pièce soit en effet la meilleure de mes tragédies. Je laisse, et aux Lecteurs, et au temps, à décider de son véritable prix. Ce que je puis assurer, c'est que je n'en ai point fait où la vertu soit plus mise en jour que dans celle-ci; les moindres fautes y sont sévèrement punies; la seule pensée du crime y est regardée avec autant d'horreur que le crime même; les faiblesses de l'amour y passent pour de vraies faiblesses; les passions

Hippolytus is accused, in Euripides, and in Seneca, of having in fact violated his stepmother: *vim corpus tulit*. But here he is only accused of having had the intention. I wished to spare Theseus a crisis of emotion which could have made him appear less sympathetic to an audience.

As for the character of Hippolytus I have noticed that among the ancients, Euripides has been reproached with having represented him as a Philosopher, exempt from all imperfections, which made the death of this young Prince give rise to more indignation than to pity. I wished to endow him with some frailty which should render him slightly guilty in his relations with his father, but which should in no way detract from that magnanimity which made him hold his tongue in order to preserve the honour of Phaedra, and which made him submit to oppression without accusing her. I call frailty that love which he feels—in spite of himself—for Aricia who is the daughter and the sister of mortal enemies of his father.

This Aricia is not a character invented by me. Virgil says that Hippolytus married her, and had, by her, a son, after he had been restored to life by Aesculapius. And I have also read certain authors who claim that Hippolytus married and led into Italy a young Athenian of noble birth, who was called Aricia, and after whom is named a small Italian town.

I mention these authorities because it has been my most scrupulous intention to follow the Legend. I have even followed the history of Theseus as it is in Plutarch.

It is in the work of this historian that I found that what had given rise to the belief that Theseus had descended into the Underworld in order to abduct Proserpina, was in fact a voyage this Prince had made in Epirus, near to the source of the river Acheron, in the kingdom of a King whose wife Pirithoüs wished to carry off, and who kept Theseus prisoner, after having put Pirithoüs to death. So I have tried to preserve the truthfulness of History without losing the adornments of the Legend which furnish so much of its poetry; and the rumour of the death of Theseus, based upon this legendary voyage, gives Phaedra the opportunity to make a declaration of love which becomes one of the chief causes of her tragedy, and which she would never have dared to make as long as she believed her husband to be living.

n'y sont présentées aux yeux que pour montrer tout le désordre dont elles sont cause; et le vice y est peint partout avec des couleurs qui en font connaître et haïr la difformité. C'est là proprement le but que tout homme qui travaille pour le public doit se proposer; et c'est ce que les premiers poètes tragiques avaient en vue sur toute chose. Leur théâtre était une école où la vertu n'était pas moins bien enseignée que dans les écoles des philosophes. Aussi Aristote a bien voulu donner des règles du poème dramatique; et Socrate, le plus sage des philosophes, ne dédaignait pas de mettre la main aux tragédies d'Euripide. Il serait à souhaiter que nos ouvrages fussent aussi solides et aussi pleins d'utiles instructions que ceux de ces poètes. Ce serait peut-être un moyen de réconcilier la tragédie avec quantité de personnes, célèbres par leur piété et par leur doctrine, qui l'ont condamnée dans ces derniers temps, et qui en jugeraient sans doute plus favorablement, si les auteurs songeaient autant à instruire leurs spectateurs qu'à les divertir, et s'ils suivaient en cela la véritable intention de la tragédie.

For the rest, I dare not yet say that this play is in fact the best of my tragedies. I leave it to my readers and to Time to decide upon its true value. But this I do say that I have written no play in which virtue has been more celebrated than in this one. The smallest faults are here severely punished; the mere idea of a crime is looked upon with as much horror as the crime itself; the weaknesses of those in love are treated as real weaknesses; passions are represented only to show all the disorder they occasion; and vice is everywhere painted in colours which render its deformity recognizable and hateful. This indeed should be the end and aim of every man who works for a public audience, and it is what the first tragic poets had in view on every subject. Their theatre was one in which virtue was no less well taught than in the schools of the philosophers. Thus Aristotle has laid down the rules for the dramatic poem; and Socrates the wisest of the philosophers did not disdain to have a hand in the tragedies of Euripides. It is to be wished that our productions might be as firmly based and as full of useful instruction as those of these poets. It might perhaps be a way of reconciling the art of the theatre with many persons, celebrated for their piety and for their learning, who have during the past few years condemned it, and who would doubt- less judge it more favourably if playwrights would study as much to instruct as to entertain their audiences, and if in this way they were to follow the true purposes of dramatic writing.

DRAMATIS PERSONAE

THESEUS	son of Ægeus, king of Athens.
PHAEDRA	wife of Theseus, daughter of Minos and Pasiphaë.
HIPPOLYTUS	son of Theseus and Antiope, queen of the Amazons.
ARICIA	princess of the Athenian blood royal.
ŒNONE	nurse and confidante of Phaedra.
THERAMENES	tutor and friend of Hippolytus.
ISMENE	confidante of Aricia.
PANOPE	a lord or lady in waiting to Phaedra.

GUARDS

The scene is Trozene, city of the Peloponnesus.

PHÈDRE

ACTE I

SCÈNE I

Hippolyte, Théramène

HIPPOLYTE

Le dessein en est pris: je pars, cher Théramène,
Et quitte le séjour de l'aimable Trézène.
Dans le doute mortel dont je suis agité,
Je commence à rougir de mon oisiveté.
Depuis plus de six mois éloigné de mon père,
J'ignore le destin d'une tête si chère;
J'ignore jusqu'aux lieux qui le peuvent cacher.

THÉRAMÈNE

Et dans quels lieux, Seigneur, l'allez-vous donc chercher?
Déjà, pour satisfaire à votre juste crainte,
J'ai couru les deux mers que sépare Corinthe;
J'ai demandé Thésée aux peuples de ces bords
Où l'on voit l'Achéron se perdre chez les morts;
J'ai visité l'Élide, et laissant le Ténare,
Passé jusqu'à la mer qui vit tomber Icare.
Sur quel espoir nouveau, dans quels heureux climats
Croyez-vous découvrir la trace de ses pas?
Qui sait même, qui sait si le Roi votre père
Veut que de son absence on sache le mystère?
Et si, lorsqu'avec vous nous tremblons pour ses jours,
Tranquille, et nous cachant de nouvelles amours,
Ce héros n'attend point qu'une amante abusée . . .

HIPPOLYTE

Cher Théramène, arrête, et respecte Thésée.
De ses jeunes erreurs désormais revenu,

ACT I

Hippolytus, Theramenes

HIPPOLYTUS

My mind's made up. I go, Theramenes:
I can no longer stay in beautiful
Trozene. In mortal doubt I waver; grow
Ashamed of idleness. Six months and more
My father has been gone! I do not know
What has become of that beloved head;
Nor even where upon the earth he hides.

THERAMENES

And in what region, Prince are you to seek?
Already, to appease your natural fears
I have traversed the seas on either side
Of Corinth; asked for news of Theseus there
Where Acheron is lost among the shades.
I tried Elis, and leaving Tœnarus,
Sailed even to that sea which saw the fall
Of Icarus. And in what happier place,
What new hope bids you find a trace of him?
Who knows, indeed who knows if he desires
The secret of his absence to be known?
Or if, while we are trembling for his life,
This hero, calmly hiding some new love,
May be awaiting a deluded girl's . . .

HIPPOLYTUS

Stop, dear Theramenes, and show respect
To Theseus. He is long returned from all

Par un indigne obstacle il n'est point retenu;
Et fixant de ses vœux l'inconstance fatale,
Phèdre depuis longtemps ne craint plus de rivale.
Enfin en le cherchant je suivrai mon devoir,
Et je fuirai ces lieux que je n'ose plus voir.

THÉRAMÈNE

Hé! depuis quand, Seigneur, craignez-vous la présence
De ces paisibles lieux, si chers à votre enfance,
Et dont je vous ai vu préférer le séjour
Au tumulte pompeux d'Athène et de la cour?
Quel péril, ou plutôt quel chagrin vous en chasse?

HIPPOLYTE

Cet heureux temps n'est plus. Tout a changé de face,
Depuis que sur ces bords les Dieux ont envoyé
La fille de Minos et de Pasiphaé.

THÉRAMÈNE

J'entends: de vos douleurs la cause m'est connue.
Phèdre ici vous chagrine, et blesse votre vue.
Dangereuse marâtre, à peine elle vous vit,
Que votre exil d'abord signala son crédit.
Mais sa haine sur vous autrefois attachée,
Ou s'est évanouie, ou s'est bien relâchée.
Et d'ailleurs quels périls vous peut faire courir
Une femme mourante et qui cherche à mourir?
Phèdre, atteinte d'un mal qu'elle s'obstine à taire,
Lasse enfin d'elle-même et du jour qui l'éclaire,
Peut-elle contre vous former quelques desseins?

HIPPOLYTE

Sa vaine inimitié n'est pas ce que je crains.

28

His youthful errors, and no obstacle
Unworthy of his fame could hold him back.
Phaedra has fixed at last a heart so long,
So fatally inconstant, and has need
No more to fear a rival. Seeking him
I shall myself only be following
The path of duty, and I shall escape,
From this place which I dare no longer see.

THERAMENES

Hey! When did you begin to dread this place
So dear to you in happy childhood, Prince?
Which you prefer, I know, to all the pomp
And tumult of th' Athenian court. What grief,
What danger do you shun?

HIPPOLYTUS

              That happy time
Is gone, Theramenes, and all is changed
Since to these shores the Gods have sent Phaedra,
Daughter of Minos and Pasiphaë.

THERAMENES

I understand your grief; I know its cause:
Her presence here offends and wounds your sight.
Your stepmother is dangerous. One look
At you and you were instantly exiled!
But now her hatred, which pursued you once,
Is either vanished, or is grown more mild.
Besides, what danger can a dying woman,
One who longs for death, bring on your head?
Can Phaedra, sick of an obscure disease
She obstinately hides, weary of life,
Herself, and of the very light of day,
Can she form any plot against you, Sir?

HIPPOLYTUS

It is not her vain enmity I fear.

29

Hippolyte en partant fuit une autre ennemie:
Je fuis, je l'avoûrai, cette jeune Aricie,
Reste d'un sang fatal conjuré contre nous.

THÉRAMÈNE

Quoi! vous-même, Seigneur, la persécutez-vous?
Jamais l'aimable sœur des cruels Pallantides
Trempa-t-elle aux complots de ses frères perfides?
Et devez-vous haïr ses innocents appas?

HIPPOLYTE

Si je la haïssais, je ne la fuirais pas.

THÉRAMÈNE

Seigneur, m'est-il permis d'expliquer votre fuite?
Pourriez-vous n'être plus ce superbe Hippolyte,
Implacable ennemi des amoureuses lois
Et d'un joug que Thésée a subi tant de fois?
Vénus, par votre orgueil si longtemps méprisée,
Voudrait-elle à la fin justifier Thésée?
Et vous mettant au rang du reste des mortels,
Vous a-t-elle forcé d'encenser ses autels?
Aimeriez-vous, Seigneur?

HIPPOLYTE

              Ami, qu'oses-tu dire?
Toi, qui connais mon cœur depuis que je respire,
Des sentiments d'un cœur si fier, si dédaigneux,
Peux-tu me demander le désaveu honteux?
C'est peu qu'avec son lait une mère amazone
M'ait fait sucer encor cet orgueil qui t'étonne;
Dans un âge plus mûr moi-même parvenu,
Je me suis applaudi quand je me suis connu.
Attaché près de moi par un zèle sincère,

In going I avoid a different foe:
I fly—if you must know, I will confess—
From that young sole survivor of a tribe
Which fatally has long conspired against
My family: Aricia.

THERAMENES

What? You?
Do you too persecute her? No, my Lord,
The gentle sister of the cruel sons
Of Pallas was no schemer in their plots.
And must you really hate her for her charm?

HIPPOLYTUS

Oh, if I hated her I should not fly.

THERAMENES

Have I permission to explain your flight?
Are you no longer proud Hippolytus,
The enemy of love, and of those laws
Obeyed so many times by Theseus?
And could it be that Venus, scorned so long
By you, has proved him, Theseus, right at last?
And, putting you with all the rest of men,
Has forced you to your knees before her shrine?
Are you in love?

HIPPOLYTUS

My friend, how dare you ask?
You who have known my heart from its first beat!
Can you expect me to disown and shame
The feelings of a heart so proud? It is
Not much perhaps that with my mother's milk
I sucked that Amazonian pride I boast,
And which amazes you, but great that when
I grew to riper years and knew myself,
I praised, myself, the self I came to know.
You who were bound, sincerely bound to me

Tu me contais alors l'histoire de mon père.
Tu sais combien mon âme, attentive à ta voix,
S'échauffait aux récits de ses nobles exploits,
Quand tu me dépeignais ce héros intrépide
Consolant les mortels de l'absence d'Alcide,
Les monstres étouffés et les brigands punis,
Procuste, Cercyon, et Scirron, et Sinnis,
Et les os dispersés du géant d'Épidaure,
Et la Crète fumant du sang du Minotaure.
Mais quand tu récitais des faits moins glorieux,
Sa foi partout offerte et reçue en cent lieux:
Hélène à ses parents dans Sparte dérobée;
Salamine témoin des pleurs de Péribée;
Tant d'autres, dont les noms lui sont même échappés,
Trop crédules esprits que sa flamme a trompés:
Ariane aux rochers contant ses injustices,
Phèdre enlevée enfin sous de meilleurs auspices;
Tu sais comme, à regret écoutant ce discours,
Je te pressais souvent d'en abréger le cours,
Heureux si j'avais pu ravir à la mémoire
Cette indigne moitié d'une si belle histoire!
Et moi-même, à mon tour, je me verrais lié?
Et les Dieux jusque-là m'auraient humilié?
Dans mes lâches soupirs d'autant plus méprisable,
Qu'un long amas d'honneurs rend Thésée excusable,
Qu'aucuns monstres par moi domptés jusqu'aujourd'hui
Ne m'ont acquis le droit de faillir comme lui.
Quand même ma fierté pourrait s'être adoucie,
Aurais-je pour vainqueur dû choisir Aricie?
Ne souviendrait-il plus à mes sens égarés
De l'obstacle éternel qui nous a séparés?
Mon père la réprouve; et par des lois sévères
Il défend de donner des neveux à ses frères:
D'une tige coupable il craint un rejeton;

In service, told me stories of my father.
You know my soul, attentive to your voice,
Kindled at hearing of his noble deeds,
When you described him, fearless and sublime,
Consoling mortals for the absence now
Of Hercules. Those monsters strangled, crushed!
The Pirates punished, and Procrustes slain;
And Cercyon, and Scirron, and Sinnis;
And Epidaurus' giant's bones dispersed!
Crete smoking with the blood of Minotaur!
But when you told me of less glorious deeds:
His promise made and broken everywhere;
Helen of Sparta, from her parents' home
Enticed by stealth; Salamis witnessing
Poor Periboëa's tears; and many more,
Too credulous creatures by his love deceived,
Whose very names he cannot now recall;
Forsaken Ariadne to the rocks
Bewailing her injustices; Phaedra
Abducted too—though less unfortunate—
You know with what regret I heard you tell,
How often begged you to cut short the tale.
How happily I would have then wiped out
The base half of so fine a history.
Am I, in turn, to find myself enslaved?
Can the Gods wish to humble me so far?
My weakness is the more contemptible
That no long list of honours and renown
Excuses me as it did Theseus.
Until today, no monsters killed by me
Have given me the right to fail like him.
And even if my pride could ever melt
Should I have been insane enough to choose
Aricia for my conqueror? Did I forget
The eternal barriers between us two?
My father disapproves; by stern command
Forbids her brothers should have sons of hers
For nephews; dreads a single shoot from stock

Il veut avec leur sœur ensevelir le nom,
Et que jusqu'au tombeau soumise à sa tutelle,
Jamais les feux d'hymen ne s'allument pour elle.
Dois-je épouser ses droits contre un père irrité?
Donnerai-je l'exemple à la témérité?
Et dans un fol amour ma jeunesse embarquée . . .

THÉRAMÈNE

Ah! Seigneur, si votre heure est une fois marquée,
Le ciel de nos raisons ne sait point s'informer.
Thésée ouvre vos yeux en voulant les fermer;
Et sa haine, irritant une flamme rebelle,
Prête à son ennemie une grâce nouvelle.
Enfin d'un chaste amour pourquoi vous effrayer?
S'il a quelque douceur, n'osez-vous l'essayer?
En croirez-vous toujours un farouche scrupule?
Craint-on de s'égarer sur les traces d'Hercule?
Quels courages Vénus n'a-t-elle point domptés?
Vous-même, où seriez-vous, vous qui la combattez,
Si toujours Antiope à ses lois opposée,
D'une pudique ardeur n'eût brûlé pour Thésée?
Mais que sert d'affecter un superbe discours?
Avouez-le, tout change; et depuis quelques jours
On vous voit moins souvent, orgueilleux et sauvage,
Tantôt faire voler un char sur le rivage,
Tantôt, savant dans l'art par Neptune inventé,
Rendre docile au frein un coursier indompté.
Les forêts de nos cris moins souvent retentissent;
Chargés d'un feu secret, vos yeux s'appesantissent.
Il n'en faut point douter: vous aimez, vous brûlez;

So guilty, and with hers, their sister's life,
Seeks to ensepulchre their name. For her,
Submissive as his ward—even to her grave—
The torch of Hymen never shall be lit.
Should I embrace her cause, and make myself
Example of foolhardiness? Against the wrath
Of an infuriated father, launch
My youth upon a course of love so mad? . . .

THERAMENES

My Lord, if once your hour is come, the Gods
Care nothing, do not wish to try to know
Of our poor reasonings! Do not you see?
Theseus in his attempt to close your eyes
Has opened them! His hate has fanned a flame
In your rebellious heart that has endowed
His enemy with glamour in your eyes.
And, after all, why should you be afraid
Of love so innocent? If it be sweet
Dare you not try its taste? Must you be ruled
For ever by the wild timidity
And scruples of a savage? Do you fear
To lose your way where Hercules has strayed?
What heart has ever been too brave to be
Vanquished by Venus? Where would you be, Sir,
Yourself, who fight her, had Antiope,
Your mother, constant in her scorn of love,
Not kindled with true love for Theseus?
What use is your pretended pride of speech?
Confess it, all is changed! These many days
You are less often seen, so proud and wild,
Making a chariot fly along the shore;
Or, practised in the art that Neptune taught,
Taming unbroken horses to the rein.
Less often do the woods return our shouts;
Your eyes are heavy, smouldering with a fire
You ill conceal. How can I doubt it now?
You love! Indeed you love! I know it. Sir!

35

Vous périssez d'un mal que vous dissimulez.
La charmante Aricie a-t-elle su vous plaire?

HIPPOLYTE

Théramène, je pars, et vais chercher mon père.

THÉRAMÈNE

Ne verrez-vous point Phèdre avant que de partir,
Seigneur?

HIPPOLYTE

C'est mon dessein: tu peux l'en avertir.
Voyons-la, puisqu'ainsi mon devoir me l'ordonne.
Mais quel nouveau malheur trouble sa chère Œnone?

SCÈNE 2

Hippolyte, Œnone, Théramène

ŒNONE

Hélas! Seigneur, quel trouble au mien peut être égal?
La Reine touche presque à son terme fatal.
En vain à l'observer jour et nuit je m'attache:
Elle meurt dans mes bras d'un mal qu'elle me cache.
Un désordre éternel règne dans son esprit.
Son chagrin inquiet l'arrache de son lit.
Elle veut voir le jour; et sa douleur profonde
M'ordonne toutefois d'écarter tout le monde . . .
Elle vient.

HIPPOLYTE

Il suffit: je la laisse en ces lieux,
Et ne lui montre point un visage odieux.

You are consumed with what you try to hide.
Has not the fair Aricia won your heart?

HIPPOLYTUS

HIPPOLYTUS

Theramenes, I go to find my father.

THERAMENES

Will you not see Phaedra before you go?

HIPPOLYTUS

That is my purpose. You may tell her so.
My duty bids me see her and I will.
But what new grief disturbs her dear Œnone?

SCENE 2

Hippolytus, Œnone, Theramenes

ŒNONE

Alas, my Lord, whose grief or tragedy
Has equalled or could ever equal mine?
The queen has almost reached her end. In vain
I watch her closely all the day and night.
She is dying in my arms, of a disease
She will not name. Disorder rules her mind.
She is dragged from bed by her tormented soul;
She must see daylight. But her agony
Is such—I must—I beg you all to go.
She comes.

HIPPOLYTUS

Enough, I leave her in this place
And show to her no more a hated face.

SCÈNE 3

Phèdre, Œnone

PHÈDRE

N'allons point plus avant. Demeurons, chère Œnone.
Je ne me soutiens plus: ma force m'abandonne.
Mes yeux sont éblouis du jour que je revoi,
Et mes genoux tremblants se dérobent sous moi.
Hélas!   (*Elle s'assied.*)

ŒNONE

Dieux tout-puissants que nos pleurs vous apaisent!

PHÈDRE

Que ces vains ornements, que ces voiles me pèsent!
Quelle importune main, en formant tous ces nœuds,
A pris soin sur mon front d'assembler mes cheveux?
Tout m'afflige et me nuit, et conspire à me nuire.

ŒNONE

Comme on voit tous ses vœux l'un l'autre se détruire!
Vous-même, condamnant vos injustes desseins,
Tantôt à vous parer vous excitiez nos mains;
Vous-même, rappelant votre force première,
Vous vouliez vous montrer et revoir la lumière.
Vous la voyez, Madame; et prête à vous cacher,
Vous haïssez le jour que vous veniez chercher?

PHÈDRE

Noble et brillant auteur d'une triste famille,
Toi, dont ma mère osait se vanter d'être fille,
Qui peut-être rouⸯis du trouble où tu me vois,
Soleil, je te viens voir pour la dernière fois.

SCENE 3

Phaedra, Œnone

PHAEDRA

No further, dear Œnone! Let us stay.
Strength ebbs away from me. I cannot stand.
My eyes are dazzled by the light of day
Suddenly seen again. My trembling knees
Give way. Ah! *(She sits.)*

ŒNONE

Would to Heaven that our tears
Might bring relief.

PHAEDRA

These useless ornaments,
These veils oppress me. What officious hands
Have taken care to knot upon my head
My heavy hair? How all conspires to hurt,
Hurt and afflict me.

ŒNONE

There you are, you see
Her wishes contradict each other! Did
You not, one moment since, condemning plans
So wicked, urge us to adorn you? Did you not,
Reviving your past strength, desire to show
Yourself, and see the light once more? You do.
So then at once you wish to hide yourself,
And hate the light you sought one moment since!

PHAEDRA

Noble and blazing Author of a race
Of sad unhappy mortals! Thou, of Whom
It was my mother's proudest boast to be
The daughter, and who well mayst blush to see
Me brought to such a pass! Oh Thou, Great Sun!
I come to look on Thee for the last time.

ŒNONE

Quoi? vous ne perdrez point cette cruelle envie?
Vous verrai-je toujours, renonçant à la vie,
Faire de votre mort les funestes apprêts?

PHÈDRE

Dieux! que ne suis-je assise à l'ombre des forêts!
Quand pourrai-je, au travers d'une noble poussière,
Suivre de l'œil un char fuyant dans la carrière?

ŒNONE

Quoi, Madame?

PHÈDRE

          Insensée, où suis-je? et qu'ai-je dit?
Où laissé-je égarer mes vœux et mon esprit?
Je l'ai perdu: les Dieux m'en ont ravi l'usage.
Œnone, la rougeur me couvre le visage:
Je te laisse trop voir mes honteuses douleurs;
Et mes yeux, malgré moi, se remplissent de pleurs.

ŒNONE

Ah! s'il vous faut rougir, rougissez d'un silence
Qui de vos maux encore aigrit la violence.
Rebelle à tous nos soins, sourde à tous nos discours,
Voulez-vous sans pitié laisser finir vos jours?
Quelle fureur les borne au milieu de leur course?
Quel charme ou quel poison en a tari la source?
Les ombres par trois fois ont obscurci les cieux
Depuis que le sommeil n'est entré dans vos yeux,
Et le jour a trois fois chassé la nuit obscure
Depuis que votre corps languit sans nourriture.
A quel affreux dessein vous laissez-vous tenter?

What! Will you not forget that cruel wish?
Am I to see you, ever, tired of life,
Preparing still your own death's remedy?

PHAEDRA

Oh why am I not sitting in the shade
Of forests? When may I follow with my eyes
That racing chariot flying down the course
Through glorious dust? . . .

ŒNONE

Madam?

PHAEDRA

Where am I? Mad?
What have I said? Where, where have I let stray
My longings, and my self-control? Œnone!
The Gods deprive me of the use of it.
I've lost it. And my face is burning red;
I blush, for I have let you see too clear
My shameful grief. Against my will my eyes
Fill up with tears.

ŒNONE

Oh! If you must blush, do!
Blush at a silence you refuse to break
Which sharpens all the time your misery's edge.
Rebellious to our care, deaf to our words,
Will you, unpitying, destroy yourself?
What fury makes you wish to end your days?
What charm or poison has dried up your source
Of life? Three times the shadows of the night
Have covered up the sky since sleep has come
Into your eyes. Three times the day has chased
The dark of night away since food has passed
Your famished lips. By what appalling plan
Are you so tempted that you dare to take

De quel droit sur vous-même osez-vous attenter?
Vous offensez les Dieux auteurs de votre vie;
Vous trahissez l'époux à qui la foi vous lie;
Vous trahissez enfin vos enfants malheureux,
Que vous précipitez sous un joug rigoureux.
Songez qu'un même jour leur ravira leur mère,
Et rendra l'espérance au fils de l'étrangère,
A ce fier ennemi de vous, de votre sang,
Ce fils qu'une Amazone a porté dans son flanc,
Cet Hippolyte . . .

PHÈDRE

Ah, Dieux!

ŒNONE

Ce reproche vous touche.

PHÈDRE

Malheureuse, quel nom est sorti de la bouche?

ŒNONE

Hé bien! votre colère éclate avec raison:
J'aime à vous voir frémir à ce funeste nom.
Vivez donc. Que l'amour, le devoir vous excite.
Vivez, ne souffrez pas que le fils d'une Scythe,
Accablant vos enfants d'un empire odieux,
Commande au plus beau sang de la Grèce et des Dieux.
Mais ne différez point: chaque moment vous tue.
Réparez promptement votre force abattue,
Tandis que de vos jours, prêts à se consumer,
Le flambeau dure encore et peut se rallumer.

Upon yourself the right of life or death?
You will offend your ancestors, the Gods,
You will betray the husband unto whom
You are bound by sacred vows. You will betray
Your miserable children too, condemned
To servitude if you forsake them. Think!
The day that takes from them their mother takes
At once their heritage and offers it
And high hopes to that foreign mother's son,
Proud enemy of you and all your race,
Him who was carried by the Amazon
Hippolytus . . .

PHAEDRA

Oh Gods!

ŒNONE

Ah, this reproach
Touches you!

PHAEDRA

Miserable fool, what name
Has passed your lips?

ŒNONE

Indeed your anger should
Explode, with reason! And I love to see
You shudder at that cursed, ill-fated name.
Then live! Let love and duty make you live!
Do not permit this Scythian's son to crush
Your lovely sons beneath his odious rule,
And so to dominate the purest blood
Of Greece and of the Gods! Make no delay!
Each instant is your murderer. Repair
At once your failing energies, while yet
Your torch of life, so nearly out, still glows,
And may perhaps be fanned into a flame.

J'en ai trop prolongé la coupable durée.

ŒNONE

Quoi? de quelques remords êtes-vous déchirée?
Quel crime a pu produire un trouble si pressant?
Vos mains n'ont point trempé dans le sang innocent?

PHÈDRE

Grâces au ciel, mes mains ne sont point criminelles.
Plût aux Dieux que mon cœur fût innocent comme elles!

ŒNONE

Et quel affreux projet avez-vous enfanté
Dont votre cœur doive être épouvanté?

PHÈDRE

Je t'en ai dit assez. Épargne-moi le reste.
Je meurs, pour ne point faire un aveu si funeste.

ŒNONE

Mourez donc, et gardez un silence inhumain;
Mais pour fermer vos yeux cherchez une autre main.
Quoiqu'il vous reste à peine une faible lumière,
Mon âme chez les morts descendra la première.
Mille chemins ouverts y conduisent toujours,
Et ma juste douleur choisira les plus courts.
Cruelle, quand ma foi vous a-t-elle déçue?
Songez-vous qu'en naissant mes bras vous ont reçue?
Mon pays, mes enfants, pour vous j'ai tout quitté.
Réserviez-vous ce prix à ma fidélité?

PHAEDRA

I have endured a guilty life too long.

ŒNONE

Why? What remorse gnaws at your heart? What crime
Can so torment you, since your hands are not
Polluted with the blood of innocence?

PHAEDRA

Thanks be to Heav'n my hands are free from stain.
I wish my soul were innocent as they.

ŒNONE

What awful project have you then conceived
So terrible it daunts your heart?

PHAEDRA

       Œnone,
I have said enough. Spare me the rest.
I die—to keep the fatal words unsaid.

ŒNONE

Die then, and keep a silence so inhuman!
Seek some other hand to close your eyes.
Although only a feeble ray of life
Remains with you, yet sure I will forestall
Your voyage to the dead, and get there first.
Always a thousand paths are open to us,
And my righteous grief shall show me how
To find the shortest cut! Oh cruelty!
When have I ever yet betrayed your faith
Or disappointed you? You were received,
Remember, into these same arms new born.
My home, my children I have left for you,
Abandoned for your sake. Is this to be
The due reward for all my loyalty?

PHÈDRE

Quel fruit espères-tu de tant de violence?
Tu frémiras d'horreur si je romps le silence.

ŒNONE

Et que me direz-vous qui ne cède, grands Dieux!
A l'horreur de vous voir expirer à mes yeux?

PHÈDRE

Quand tu sauras mon crime, et le sort qui m'accable,
Je n'en mourrai pas moins, j'en mourrai plus coupable.

ŒNONE

Madame, au nom des pleurs que pour vous j'ai versés,
Par vos faibles genoux que je tiens embrassés,
Délivrez mon esprit de ce funeste doute.

PHÈDRE

Tu le veux. Lève toi.

ŒNONE

Parlez, je vous écoute.

PHÈDRE

Ciel! que lui vais-je dire, et par où commencer?

ŒNONE

Par de vaines frayeurs cessez de m'offenser.

PHÈDRE

O haine de Vénus! O fatale colère!
Dans quels égarements l'amour jeta ma mère!

PHAEDRA

What answer can you hope to gain by force?
If I break silence you will shake with horror.

ŒNONE

What can you tell me—Gods in Heaven above!—
To horrify me more than what I see?
You dying here and now before my eyes!

PHAEDRA

When you shall know my crime and heavy fate
I shall not die the less. I shall still die
But blamed for ever.

ŒNONE

          Madam, by my tears,
These many tears I've shed for you; your knees,
These feeble knees I clasp, deliver me
From hellish doubt!

PHAEDRA

          It is you who insist.
Get up then.

ŒNONE

         Tell me. I am listening. Speak.

PHAEDRA

Heavens! What am I to tell her? Where begin?

ŒNONE

Oh cease to vex me with your childish fears.

PHAEDRA

Your fatal hatred Venus! Oh, your wrath!
Into what aberrations did Love cast
My mother!

47

OENONE

Oublions-les, Madame; et qu'à tout l'avenir
Un silence éternel cache ce souvenir.

PHÈDRE

Ariane, ma sœur, de quel amour blessée,
Vous mourûtes aux bords où vous fûtes laissée!

OENONE

Que faites-vous, Madame? et quel mortel ennui
Contre tout votre sang vous anime aujourd'hui?

PHÈDRE

Puisque Vénus le veut, de ce sang déplorable
Je péris la dernière et la plus misérable.

OENONE

Aimez-vous?

PHÉDRE

De l'amour j'ai toutes les fureurs.

OENONE

Pour qui?

PHÈDRE

Tu vas ouïr le comble des horreurs.
J'aime ... A ce nom fatal, je tremble, ie frissonne,
J'aime ...

OENONE

Qui?

48

ŒNONE

Let such stories be forgot,
And deep in silence be for ever lost.

PHAEDRA

Ariadne, my sister, by what Love
Were you wounded and left to die alone
Upon that shore!

ŒNONE

Madam, what do you mean?
What special grief makes you complain today
So bitterly of all your family?

PHAEDRA

Since Venus wills it so, I perish now,
Of that doomed family, the last and most
Pitiable.

ŒNONE

Are you in love?

PHAEDRA

I feel
All love's wild ecstasies.

ŒNONE

For whom?

PHAEDRA

Now hear
The crowning horror. Yes, I love—I shake
I tremble at his very name—I love . . .

ŒNONE

Whom?

Tu connais ce fils de l'Amazone,
Ce prince si longtemps par moi-même opprimé?

OENONE

Hippolyte? Grands Dieux!

PHÈDRE

C'est toi qui l'a nommé.

OENONE

Juste ciel! tout mon sang dans mes veines se glace.
O désespoir! ô crime! ô déplorable race!
Voyage infortuné! Rivage malheureux,
Fallait-il approcher de tes bords dangereux?

PHÈDRE

Mon mal vient de plus loin. A peine au fils d'Égée
Sous les lois de l'hymen je m'étais engagée,
Mon repos, mon bonheur semblait être affermi;
Athènes me montra mon superbe ennemi.
Je le vis, je rougis, je pâlis à sa vue;
Un trouble s'éleva dans mon âme éperdue;
Mes yeux ne voyaient plus, je ne pouvais parler;
Je sentis tout mon corps et transir et brûler.
Je reconnus Vénus et ses feux redoutables,
D'un sang qu'elle poursuit tourments inévitables.
Par des vœux assidus je crus les détourner:
Je lui bâtis un temple, et pris soin de l'orner.
De victimes moi-même à toute heure entourée,
Je cherchais dans leurs flancs ma raison égarée.
D'un incurable amour remèdes impuissants!
En vain sur les autels ma main brûlait l'encens:
Quand ma bouche implorait le nom de la Déesse,
J'adorais Hippolyte; et le voyant sans cesse,

PHAEDRA

You know him, son of the Amazon,
That Prince whom I myself have for so long
Oppressed.

ŒNONE

Hippolytus! Great Gods!

PHAEDRA

It's you
Have named him!

ŒNONE

Oh despair! Great Heavens, my blood
Now freezes in my veins! Oh cursed race!
Oh crime! Unhappy land, reached at the end
Of what ill fated voyage! Why were we
Doomed ever to approach your dangerous shores!

PHAEDRA

This malady of mine is from far back.
Only just married to Aegeus' son,
My peace, my happiness seemed safe at last,
When Athens showed me my proud enemy.
I saw him. First I blushed and then grew pale;
At sight of him my troubled soul was lost.
My eyes no longer saw, I could not speak;
I felt my blood run icy and then burn;
I recognized Her! Venus! Dreaded fires,
Inevitable torments for that blood
Which She pursues. With fervent vows I thought
To ward them off: I built for Her a Shrine,
Adorned it with great care, and at all hours,
Myself surrounded by my victims, sought
In their entrails the reason I had lost.
Weak remedies for love incurable!
In vain my hand burnt incense at Her shrine
My mouth invoked Her name, my heart adored

51

Même au pied des autels que je faisais fumer,
J'offrais tout à ce dieu que je n'osais nommer.
Je l'évitais partout. O comble de misère!
Mes yeux le retrouvaient dans les traits de son père.
Contre moi-même enfin j'osai me révolter:
J'excitai mon courage à le persécuter.
Pour bannir l'ennemi dont j'étais idolâtre,
J'affectai les chagrins d'une injuste marâtre;
Je pressai son exil, et mes cris éternels
L'arrachèrent du sein et des bras paternels.
Je respirais, Œnone; et depuis son absence,
Mes jours moins agités coulaient dans l'innocence.
Soumise à mon époux, et cachant mes ennuis,
De son fatal hymen je cultivais les fruits.
Vaines précautions! Cruelle destinée!
Par mon époux lui-même à Trézène amenée,
J'ai revu l'ennemi que j'avais éloigné:
Ma blessure trop vive aussitôt a saigné.
Ce n'est plus une ardeur dans mes veines cachée:
C'est Vénus toute entière à sa proie attachée.
J'ai conçu pour mon crime une juste terreur;
J'ai pris la vie en haine, et ma flamme en horreur.
Je voulais en mourant prendre soin de ma gloire,
Et dérober au jour une flamme si noire:
Je n'ai pu soutenir tes larmes, tes combats;
Je t'ai tout avoué; je ne m'en repens pas,
Pourvu que de ma mort respectant les approches,
Tu ne m'affliges plus par d'injustes reproches,
Et que tes vains secours cessent de rappeler
Un reste de chaleur tout prêt à s'exhaler.

Hippolytus; and, always seeing him,
Continually, even at the foot
Of altars that I made to smoke for Her,
Worshipped the god whose name I dared not speak.
I fled his presence everywhere, but found him—
Crowning misery!—in his father's face!
Against myself at last I dared revolt,
And forced myself to persecute my love,
My foe whom I adored. To banish him
I feign'd a stepmother's malevolence
And for his unjust exile pressed so hard,
With such incessant clamour that at last,
I tore him from his father's heart and arms.
I breathed again, Œnone, once again,
With him away, my days were innocent.
I could submit to Theseus, hide my grief,
Devote myself to bringing up the sons
Of such a fatal marriage. All in vain!
Brought here to Trozene by my lord himself
I had to see the enemy I shunned,
And my live wound instantly bled afresh.
No longer is it fever of the blood
Concealed within my veins, but She, herself,
Venus herself, entire, crouched on her prey.
Now I am seized with terror for my crime;
I hate my life; my love is horrible.
I wish, in dying, to preserve my fame,
And hide from light of day a love so black.
But I have been unable to withstand
Your tears and supplications. I have told
You all, without regret, if only you
Will give me leave to die and cease to plague
Me with unjust reproaches; cease your vain
Attempts to fan back into flame a spark
Of life now almost out.

SCÈNE 4

Phèdre, Œnone, Panope

PANOPE

Je voudrais vous cacher une triste nouvelle,
Madame; mais il faut que je vous la révèle.
La mort vous a ravi votre invincible époux;
Et ce malheur n'est plus ignoré que de vous.

ŒNONE

Panope, que dis-tu?

PANOPE

        Que la Reine abusée
En vain demande au ciel le retour de Thésée;
Et que par des vaisseaux arrivés dans le port
Hippolyte, son fils, vient d'apprendre sa mort.

PHÈDRE

Ciel!

PANOPE

        Pour le choix d'un maître Athènes se partage.
Au Prince votre fils l'un donne son suffrage,
Madame; et de l'État l'autre oubliant les lois,
Au fils de l'étrangère ose donner sa voix.
On dit même qu'au trône une brigue insolente
Veut placer Aricie et le sang de Pallante.
J'ai cru de ce péril vous devoir avertir.
Déjà même Hippolyte est tout prêt à partir;
Et l'on craint, s'il paraît dans ce nouvel orage,
Qu'il n'entraîne après lui tout un peuple volage.

SCENE 4

Phaedra, Œnone, Panope

PANOPE

            I wish I might
Conceal the news I bring, for it is sad,
Your Majesty, but it must be revealed.
Your husband, your unconquerable lord
Has been struck down by death, and you alone
Are last to hear of this disaster.

ŒNONE

                          What
Is this you say, Panope?

PANOPE

                  That the Queen
Is vainly asking Heaven to send him back,
When, from the ships just now come into port,
Hippolytus his son learns of his death!

PHAEDRA

Oh Gods!

PANOPE

              For choice of master Athens now
Divides itself; some to the Prince your son
Are loyal, Madam; others, letting go
Allegiance to the laws of state, have dared
To vote for him, the foreign mother's son.
It's even said that a rebellious group
Intend to place Aricia and her line
Of Pallantides on the throne! I thought
I ought to warn you of this danger. Now
Hippolytus already is prepared
To leave; and if in this new turbulence
He should appear, we fear the fickle crowd
Would follow such a leader to a man.

Panope, c'est assez. La Reine, qui t'entend,
Ne négligera point cet avis important.

SCÈNE 5

Phèdre, Œnone

ŒNONE

Madame, je cessais de vous presser de vivre;
Déjà même au tombeau je songeais à vous suivre;
Pour vous en détourner je n'avais plus de voix;
Mais ce nouveau malheur vous prescrit d'autres lois.
Votre fortune change et prend une autre face:
Le Roi n'est plus, Madame; il faut prendre sa place.
Sa mort vous laisse un fils à qui vous vous devez,
Esclave s'il vous perd, et roi si vous vivez.
Sur qui, dans son malheur, voulez-vous qu'il s'appuie?
Ses larmes n'auront plus de main qui les essuie;
Et ses cris innocents, portés jusques aux Dieux,
Iront contre sa mère irriter ses aïeux.
Vivez, vous n'avez plus de reproche à vous faire.
Votre flamme devient une flamme ordinaire.
Thésée en expirant vient de rompre les nœuds
Qui faisaient tout le crime et l'horreur de vos feux.
Hippolyte pour vous devient moins redoutable;
Et vous pouvez le voir sans vous rendre coupable.
Peut-être, convaincu de votre aversion,
Il va donner un chef à la sédition.
Détrompez son erreur, fléchissez son courage.
Roi de ces bords heureux, Trézène est son partage.
Mais il sait que les lois donnent à votre fils
Les superbes remparts que Minerve a bâtis.
Vous avez l'un et l'autre une juste ennemie:

Enough, Panope. That will do. The Queen
Who hears your message will not risk neglect
Of such momentous news. You may withdraw.

SCENE 5

Phaedra, Œnone

ŒNONE

Madame, I ceased to urge that you should live;
I thought to follow you into the grave
From which I had no more the heart to turn you;
But this new blow prescribes for you new laws:
Your fortune changes, shows a different face.
The King is dead. My Lady, you must take
His place. His death leaves you a son to whom
You owe yourself: slave, if he loses you;
King if you live! On whom do you suppose
Could he, in such misfortune, lean? No hand
Would wipe away his tears. His innocent cries,
Mounting to Heav'n will irritate the Gods,
His ancestors, against his mother. Live!
Madam, you need no more reproach yourself.
Your love becomes an ordinary love!
By Theseus' death all knots have been untied
Which made your love a horror and a crime.
You need no longer fear Hippolytus;
And you may see him now without reproach.
Perhaps, convinced you are his enemy
He means to lead the rebels. Change his mind!
Show him his error. Soften his intent.
King of these fertile shores indeed he is;
Trozene is his undoubted heritage,
But well he knows the law gives to your son
The ramparts of Minerva's citadel.
You justly share a common enemy!

Unissez-vous tous deux pour combattre Aricie.

PHÈDRE

Hé bien! à tes conseils je me laisse entraîner.
Vivons, si vers la vie on peut me ramener,
Et si l'amour, d'un fils en ce moment funeste
De mes faibles esprits peut ranimer le reste.

Unite! Take hands the two of you to fight
Aricia.

PHAEDRA

By your counsels I allow
Myself to be dragged back to life. I will
Yes, I will live, if life can be restored;
If love for my dear son still has the pow'r
To rouse my failing spirit in this hour.

ACTE II

SCÈNE I

Aricie, Ismène

ARICIE

Hippolyte demande à me voir en ce lieu?
Hippolyte me cherche, et veut me dire adieu?
Ismène, dis-tu vrai? N'es-tu point abusée?

ISMÈNE

C'est le premier effet de la mort de Thésée.
Préparez-vous, Madame, à voir de tous côtés
Voler vers vous les cœurs par Thésée écartés.
Aricie à la fin de son sort est maîtresse,
Et bientôt à ses pieds verra toute la Grèce.

ARICIE

Ce n'est donc point, Ismène, un bruit mal affermi?
Je cesse d'être esclave, et n'ai plus d'ennemi?

ISMÈNE

Non, Madame, les Dieux ne vous sont plus contraires;
Et Thésée a rejoint les mânes de vos frères.

ARICIE

Dit-on quelle aventure a terminé ses jours?

ISMÈNE

On sème de sa mort d'incroyables discours.
On dit que ravisseur d'une amante nouvelle,

ACT II

SCENE I

Aricia, Ismene

ARICIA

Hippolytus has asked to see me here?
Hippolytus asked you to seek me out?
To bid farewell? Is this the truth, Ismene?
And are you sure that you are not deceived?

ISMENE

This is the first result of Theseus' death.
Prepare yourself to see from every side
Those hearts fly to you that were kept away
By Theseus. Now Aricia, at last,
At long last, is the mistress of her fate
And she shall soon see all Greece at her feet.

ARICIA

It is not then a baseless rumour, dear
Ismene? Am I then no longer slave?
And can it be I have no enemies?

ISMENE

The Gods are not against you any more!
Theseus is gone to join your brothers' ghosts.

ARICIA

Do they report what put an end to him?

ISMENE

Wild rumours of his death are spread about.
Some say that seeking, in his usual way,

Les flots ont englouti cet époux infidèle.
On dit même, et ce bruit est partout répandu,
Qu'avec Pirithoüs aux enfers descendu,
Il a vu le Cocyte et les rivages sombres,
Il s'est montré vivant aux infernales ombres;
Mais qu'il n'a pu sortir de ce triste séjour,
Et repasser les bords qu'on passe sans retour.

ARICIE

Croirai-je qu'un mortel, avant sa dernière heure,
Peut pénétrer des morts la profonde demeure?
Quel charme l'attirait sur ces bords redoutés?

ISMÈNE

Thésée est mort, Madame, et vous seule en doutez.
Athènes en gémit, Trézène en est instruite,
Et déjà pour son roi reconnaît Hippolyte.
Phèdre, dans ce palais, tremblante pour son fils,
De ses amis troublés demande les avis.

ARICIE

Et tu crois que pour moi plus humain que son père,
Hippolyte rendra ma chaîne plus légère?
Qu'il plaindra mes malheurs?

ISMÈNE

Madame, je le croi.

ARICIE

L'insensible Hippolyte est-il connu de toi?
Sur quel frivole espoir penses-tu qu'il me plaigne,

To ravish a new love this 'great untruth
Of love' was swallowed by the waves! Some say—
And this report is commonly believed—
That he, with Pirithoüs, to the world
Below descended, saw the gloomy shores
Of dark Cocytus, and himself, alive,
Appeared before the ghosts in Hell! but that
He could not then return from that sad place
Where entering means departing nevermore.

ARICIA

Can I believe that any mortal could
Before his last breath, penetrate the deep
Realm of the Dead? What charm could draw a man
To territory so redoubtable?

ISMENE

Theseus is dead, my lady, you alone
Still doubt it. Athens groans at it. Trozene
Knows it and hails Hippolytus as king.
Already Phaedra, trembling for her son,
Is seeking counsel in this palace now
From friends as anxious as herself.

ARICIA

                        And will
Hippolytus prove kinder, do you think,
To me, than Theseus? Make my chains more light?
And pity my unhappiness?

ISMENE

                    He will.
I do believe it, Madam, yes.

ARICIA

                    Do you
Then know this celebrated rock? Do you?
How can you be so simple as to hope

Et respecte en moi seule un sexe qu'il dédaigne?
Tu vois depuis quel temps il évite nos pas,
Et cherche tous les lieux où nous ne sommes pas.

ISMÈNE

Je sais de ses froideurs tout ce que l'on récite;
Mais j'ai vu près de vous ce superbe Hippolyte;
Et même, en le voyant, le bruit de sa fierté
A redoublé pour lui ma curiosité.
Sa présence à ce bruit n'a pas paru répondre:
Dès vos premiers regards je l'ai vu se confondre.
Ses yeux qui vainement voulaient vous éviter,
Déjà pleins de langueur, ne pouvaient vous quitter.
Le nom d'amant peut-être offense son courage;
Mais il en a les yeux, s'il n'en a le langage.

ARICIE

Que mon cœur, chère Ismène, écoute avidement
Un discours qui peut-être a peu de fondement!
O toi qui me connais, te semblait-il croyable
Que le triste jouet d'un sort impitoyable,
Un cœur toujours nourri d'amertume et de pleurs,
Dût connaître l'amour et ses folles douleurs?
Reste du sang d'un roi, noble fils de la terre,
Je suis seule échappée aux fureurs de la guerre.
J'ai perdu, dans la fleur de leur jeune saison,
Six frères . . . Quel espoir d'une illustre maison!
Le fer moissonna tout; et la terre humectée
But à regret le sang des neveux d'Erechthée.
Tu sais, depuis leur mort, quelle sévère loi
Défend à tous les Grecs de soupirer pour moi:
On craint que de la sœur les flammes téméraires
Ne raniment un jour la cendre de ses frères.

That he might pity and respect in me,
In me alone a sex which he disdains?
You know how he avoids us—always has—
And only likes to be where we are not.

I know the tales they tell of him: so cold!
But I have seen this proud Hippolytus
Near you, and seeing him, his pride's renown
Redoubled curiosity in me.
In fact his presence did not seem to fit
The tales I'd heard of him. At your first look
I saw him flustered, and confused. His eyes,
Which vainly tried to turn away from you,
Were anchored fast in languor, could not move!
He may not like it said he is in love;
He has the looks of it, if not the tongue!

ARICIA

How hungrily my heart hears what you say,
Though it may be without foundation.
Did it seem credible to you who know me
That the sad toy of a relentless fate,
This heart whose daily nourishment has been
Anguish and bitter tears, should ever know
Love, and the foolish agonies of love?
Last offspring of a King, the noble son
Of Earth, I was the only one survived
The fury of the war. And I have lost,
In their young season, in their spring, their spring,
Six brothers! Hope of an illustrious house,
Mown by the sword, the sons of Erectheus,
Whose blood the sodden earth sopped up with grief.
You know, only too well, how since their death,
The most severe decree has made it law
That no Greek heart may beat, or sigh, for me.
Lest by a sister's love's temerity
The brothers' ashes be perchance relit.

65

Mais tu sais bien aussi de quel œil dédaigneux
Je regardais ce soin d'un vainqueur soupçonneux.
Tu sais que de tout temps à l'amour opposée,
Je rendais souvent grâce à l'injuste Thésée,
Dont l'heureuse rigueur secondait mes mépris.
Mes yeux alors, mes yeux n'avaient pas vu son fils.
Non que par les yeux seuls lâchement enchantée,
J'aime en lui sa beauté, sa grâce tant vantée,
Présents dont la nature a voulu l'honorer,
Qu'il méprise lui-même, et qu'il semble ignorer.
J'aime, je prise en lui de plus nobles richesses,
Les vertus de son père, et non point les faiblesses.
J'aime, je l'avouerai, cet orgueil généreux
Qui jamais n'a fléchi sous le joug amoureux.
Phèdre en vain s'honorait des soupirs de Thésée:
Pour moi, je suis plus fière, et fuis la gloire aisée
D'arracher un hommage à mille autres offert,
Et d'entrer dans un cœur de toutes parts ouvert.
Mais de faire fléchir un courage inflexible,
De porter la douleur dans une âme insensible,
D'enchaîner un captif de ses fers étonné,
Contre un joug qui lui plaît vainement mutiné:
C'est là ce que je veux, c'est là ce qui m'irrite;
Hercule à désarmer coûtait moins qu'Hippolyte;
Et vaincu plus souvent, et plus tôt surmonté,
Préparait moins de gloire aux yeux qui l'ont dompté.
Mais, chère Ismène, hélas! quelle est mon imprudence!
On ne m'opposera que trop de résistance.
Tu m'entendras peut-être, humble dans mon ennui,
Gémir du même orgueil que j'admire aujourd'hui.
Hippolyte aimerait? Par quel bonheur extrême
Aurais-je pu fléchir . . .

You know, besides, with what disdain I viewed
These laws of a suspicious conqueror.
You know that I have always been opposed
To love and therefore often rendered thanks
To unjust Theseus, whose severity
Happily reinforced my own contempt!
But then my eyes, my eyes had never yet
Beheld his son. Not that my eyes alone,
Weakly attracted, made me love in him
A celebrated grace and beauty: gifts
Bestowed on him by Nature and of which
He seems unconscious, or indeed to scorn:
I love in him a richer, rarer prize
His father's strength without his weaknesses.
I love, I own I love, that noble pride
Which never yet has stooped to be in love.
Phaedra won little glory from the love
Of Theseus. I, more proud, refuse to snatch
The easy triumph of such lavish vows,
A thousand times elsewhere bestowed, and shun
A love whose heart's an ever-open door!
But to make stoop a heart inflexible;
To touch a soul insensible to love;
To take a captive startled by his chains,
Vainly a mutineer against his joy,
That is my heart's desire, that is my spur!
Even Hercules was easier to disarm
Than this Hippolytus, for he gave in
More often and more quickly, and so laid
A lesser triumph at the feet of her,
Each her he vanquished! But, my dear Ismene,
How rash I am, for I shall find opposed
To me resistance far too strong, alas!
And you may hear me, humbled in defeat,
Groan under that same pride I now admire.
What? Can he be in love? Hippolytus?
And can it be my heaven to be ...

Vous l'entendrez lui-même:
Il vient à vous.

SCÈNE 2

Hippolyte, Aricie, Ismène

HIPPOLYTE

Madame, avant que de partir,
J'ai cru de votre sort vous devoir avertir.
Mon père ne vit plus. Ma juste défiance
Présageait les raisons de sa trop longue absence.
La mort seule, bornant ses travaux éclatants,
Pouvait à l'univers le cacher si longtemps.
Les Dieux livrent enfin à la Parque homicide
L'ami, le compagnon, le successeur d'Alcide.
Je crois que votre haine, épargnant ses vertus,
Écoute sans regret ces noms qui lui sont dus.
Un espoir adoucit ma tristesse mortelle:
Je puis vous affranchir d'une austère tutelle.
Je révoque des lois dont j'ai plaint la rigueur.
Vous pouvez disposer de vous, de votre cœur;
Et dans cette Trézène, aujourd'hui mon partage,
De mon aïeul Pitthée autrefois l'héritage,
Qui m'a, sans balancer, reconnu pour son roi,
Je vous laisse aussi libre, et plus libre que moi.

ARICIE

Modérez des bontés dont l'excès m'embarrasse.
D'un soin si généreux honorer ma disgrâce,
Seigneur, c'est me ranger, plus que vous en pensez,
Sous ces austères lois dont vous me dispensez.

You shall
Yourself at once hear what he has to say
For here he comes.

SCENE 2

Hippolytus, Aricia, Ismene

HIPPOLYTUS

Madam, before I go
I think I ought to tell you of your fate.
My father's dead; my worst fears prophesied
The reason for his absence so prolonged;
That death alone, curbing his high exploits
Could hide him from the universe so long.
The Gods at last have doomed him, even him
Alcides' friend, companion, and successor,
To the homicidal shears of Fate.
I think your hatred, tempered to his virtues
May hear without resentment words like these
Of praise which he deserves. One hope consoles
My mortal grief; for I can set you free.
I here revoke that rigorous decree
Which always made me pity you. You are
At your own disposition, heart and hand;
And in Trozene, today my heritage,
Where once reigned Pittheus, my ancestor
And which has recognized me now as King,
I leave you free, more free than I myself.

ARICIA

Oh be less lavish with your kindness, Sir!
To honour thus my state of servitude
Is to embarrass me and bind me more
Than you can think to those harsh laws from which
It seems it is your wish to set me free.

Du choix d'un successeur Athènes incertaine
Parle de vous, me nomme, et le fils de la Reine.

ARICIE

De moi, Seigneur?

HIPPOLYTE

Je sais, sans vouloir me flatter,
Qu'une superbe loi semble me rejeter.
La Grèce me reproche une mère étrangère.
Mais si pour concurrent je n'avais que mon frère,
Madame, j'ai sur lui de véritables droits
Que je saurais sauver du caprice des lois.
Un frein plus légitime arrête mon audace:
Je vous cède ou plutôt je vous rends une place,
Un sceptre que jadis vos aïeux ont reçu
De ce fameux mortel que la terre a conçu.
L'adoption le mit entre les mains d'Égée.
Athènes, par mon père accrue et protégée,
Reconnut avec joie un roi si généreux,
Et laissa dans l'oubli vos frères malheureux.
Athènes dans ses murs maintenant vous rappelle.
Assez elle a gémi d'une longue querelle;
Assez dans ses sillons votre sang englouti
A fait fumer le champ dont il était sorti.
Trézène m'obéit. Les campagnes de Crète
Offrent au fils de Phèdre une riche retraite.
L'Attique est votre bien. Je pars, et vais pour vous
Réunir tous les vœux partagés entre nous.

ARICIE

De tout ce que j'entends étonnée et confuse,
Je crains presque, je crains qu'un songe ne m'abuse.

Athens, uncertain how to fill the throne,
Speaks now of you, of me, and of the son
Of Phaedra.

ARICIA

Speaks of me, my Lord?

HIPPOLYTUS

I know
The unflattering truth is that I am, it seems,
Rejected by a too proud law's decree.
Greece counts my foreign mother a reproach.
But if my brother were my only rival
My rights prevail so clearly over his
That I should save them from the laws' caprice.
My enterprise is checked by claims more just.
To you I yield my place, or rather own
That it is yours by right, and yours the sceptre
Handed down to your own ancestors
By that first famous mortal, Son of Earth.
Adoption placed it in the hands of Ægeus;
Then, Athens, by my father's strength preserved,
Protected and increased, welcomed with joy
A King so generous; and left, alas,
Your luckless brothers in oblivion.
Now she invites you back within her walls.
So long a quarrel has cost groans enough.
Her furrows are soaked deep with blood of yours,
Steaming from fields from which it sprung at first.
Trozene obeys me: and the plains of Crete
Are kingdom rich enough for Phaedra's son.
Athens is yours. I go at once to join
For you the votes divided now between us.

ARICIA

Astonished and confused by all I hear,
I fear, I almost fear a dream deceives me.

71

Veillé-je? Puis-je croire un semblable dessein?
Quel Dieu, Seigneur, quel Dieu l'a mis dans votre sein?
Qu'à bon droit votre gloire en tous lieux est semée!
Et que la vérité passe la renommée!
Vous-même, en ma faveur, vous voulez vous trahir?
N'était-ce point assez de ne me point haïr,
Et d'avoir si longtemps pu défendre votre âme
De cette inimitié . . .

HIPPOLYTE

Moi, vous haïr, Madame?
Avec quelques couleurs qu'on ait peint ma fierté,
Croit-on que dans ses flancs un monstre m'ait porté?
Quelles sauvages mœurs, quelle haine endurcie
Pourrait, en vous voyant, n'être point adoucie?
Ai-je pu résister au charme décevant . . .

ARICIE

Quoi? Seigneur.

HIPPOLYTE

Je me suis engagé trop avant.
Je vois que la raison cède à la violence.
Puisque j'ai commencé de rompre le silence,
Madame, il faut poursuivre: il faut vous informer
D'un secret que mon cœur ne peut plus renfermer.
Vous voyez devant vous un prince déplorable,
D'un téméraire orgueil exemple mémorable.
Moi qui, contre l'amour fièrement révolté,
Aux fers de ses captifs ai longtemps insulté;
Qui des faibles mortels déplorant les naufrages,
Pensais toujours du bord contempler les orages;
Asservi maintenant sous la commune loi,
Par quel trouble me vois-je emporté loin de moi!
Un moment a vaincu mon audace imprudente:
Cette âme si superbe est enfin dépendante.
Depuis près de six mois, honteux, désespéré,

Am I indeed awake? Can I believe
In such a plan? What God, my Lord, what God
Has put it in your heart? How well deserved
Is your renown throughout the world! How far
The truth outstrips that fair renown! Would you,
To favour me, prove traitor to yourself?
Was it not kind enough never to hate me?
And to have kept yourself so long aloof
From enmity which . . .

HIPPOLYTUS

                Hate you? I to hate you?
However darkly my fierce pride was painted
Do you suppose a monster gave me birth?
What savage manners, hardened temper, could
Or would not soften at the sight of you?
Could I resist a charm so innocent . . .

ARICIA

Why, what is this, Sir?

HIPPOLYTUS

                I have said too much
Not to say more. Reason I see gives in
To violence of passion. I have broken
Silence at last, and I must tell you now
The secret that my heart can hold no more.
You see before you an unhappy case
Of hasty pride, a prince who claims compassion.
I, who so long the enemy of love,
Mocked at his fetters and despised his slaves,
Who, pitying poor shipwrecked mortals, thought
Always from a safe shore to view their storms,
Now find myself subject to that same law.
By what storm do I see myself whirled off!
One moment vanquished all my foolish pride;
My so proud soul is now a suppliant.
For six months past, ashamed and desperate,

73

Portant partout le trait dont je suis déchiré,
Contre vous, contre moi, vainement je m'éprouve:
Présente, je vous fuis; absente, je vous trouve;
Dans le fond des forêts votre image me suit;
La lumière du jour, les ombres de la nuit,
Tout retrace à mes yeux les charmes que j'évite;
Tous vous livre à l'envi le rebelle Hippolyte.
Moi-même, pour tout fruit de mes soins superflus,
Maintenant je me cherche et ne me trouve plus.
Mon arc, mes javelots, mon char, tout m'importune;
Je ne me souviens plus des leçons de Neptune;
Mes seuls gémissements font retentir les bois,
Et mes coursiers oisifs ont oublié ma voix.
Peut-être le récit d'un amour si sauvage
Vous fait, en m'écoutant, rougir de votre ouvrage.
D'un cœur qui s'offre à vous quel farouche entretien!
Quel étrange captif pour un si beau lien!
Mais l'offrande à vos yeux en doit être plus chère.
Songez que je vous parle une langue étrangère;
Et ne rejetez pas des vœux mal exprimés,
Qu'Hippolyte sans vous n'aurait jamais formés.

SCÈNE 3

Hippolyte, Aricie, Théramène, Ismène

THÉRAMÈNE

Seigneur, la Reine vient, et je l'ai devancée.
Elle vous cherche.

HIPPOLYTE

Moi?

74

Carrying everywhere the shaft that splits
My heart, I struggle vainly to be free
From you and from myself. I shun you present;
Absent I find you near. Your image haunts
Me in the forest's depth. The light of day,
The shades of night, all bring back to my view
The charms that I avoid; all things conspire
To make rebellious Hippolytus
Your willing slave; and what is more, myself—
For fruit of all my endless futile search—
I can no longer even find myself!
My bow, my chariot, my javelins
Bore me. But worse. I find I have forgot
All lessons taught by Neptune! Only groans
Not shouts of mine re-echo through the woods;
My lazy stallions have forgot my voice.
Perhaps this tale of passion so uncouth
Makes you, in hearing me, blush at your work.
How wild a way to offer you a heart!
How strange a captive for so beautiful
A leash! But dearer to your eyes should be
This offering. Believe I speak a tongue
Unknown to me! Do not reject these vows
So ill-expressed, indeed, which, but for you,
I never would have formed at all.

SCENE 3

Hippolytus, Theramenes, Aricia, Ismene

THERAMENES

                              The Queen
Approaches, Prince, and I am sent before
To tell you it is you she seeks.

HIPPOLYTUS

                         What me?

THÉRAMÈNE

J'ignore sa pensée.
Mais on vous est venu demander de sa part.
Phèdre veut vous parler avant votre départ.

HIPPOLYTE

Phèdre? Que lui dirai-je? Et que peut-elle attendre . . .

ARICIE

Seigneur, vous ne pouvez refuser de l'entendre.
Quoique trop convaincu de son inimitié,
Vous devez à ses pleurs quelque ombre de pitié.

HIPPOLYTE

Cependant vous sortez. Et je pars. Et j'ignore
Si je n'offense point les charmes que j'adore!
J'ignore si ce cœur que je laisse en vos mains . . .

ARICIE

Partez, Prince, et suivez vos généreux desseins.
Rendez de mon pouvoir Athènes tributaire.
J'accepte tous les dons que vous me voulez faire.
Mais cet empire enfin si grand, si glorieux,
N'est pas de vos présents le plus cher à mes yeux.

SCÈNE 4

Hippolyte, Théramène

HIPPOLYTE

Ami, tout est-il prêt? Mais la Reine s'avance.
Va, que pour le départ tout s'arme en diligence.
Fais donner le signal, cours, ordonne, et revien
Me délivrer bientôt d'un fâcheux entretien.

THERAMENES

Yes. What her thought may be I do not know
But I am sent on her behalf, to say:
Phaedra would speak with you before you go.

HIPPOLYTUS

Phaedra? What shall I say to her? And what
Can she expect?

THERAMENES

          You cannot, Prince, refuse
To hear her, even though you are convinced
She is your enemy; for to her tears
You must accord some shade of sympathy.

HIPPOLYTUS

But wait! You go; and I too. Will you let
Us part thus? Leaving me in ignorance
Whether I have offended her I love?
Whether my heart, left in your hands . . .

ARICIA

Go, Prince, pursue your generous designs:
Make Athens tributary to my power.
All gifts you offer me I will accept,
But that proud empire, glorious though it be
Is not the one most precious unto me.

SCENE 4

Hippolytus, Theramenes

HIPPOLYTUS

Friend, is all ready? But look, here's the Queen!
Prepare at once for our departure. Go,
Give orders, signals, hasten and return,
To free me from this tiresome interview.

77

SCÈNE 5

Phèdre, Hippolyte, Œnone

PHÈDRE

Le voici. Vers mon cœur tout mon sang se retire.
J'oublie, en le voyant, ce que je viens lui dire.

ŒNONE

Souvenez-vous d'un fils qui n'espère qu'en vous.

PHÈDRE

On dit qu'un prompt départ vous éloigne de nous,
Seigneur. A vos douleurs je viens joindre mes larmes.
Je vous viens pour un fils expliquer mes alarmes.
Mon fils n'a plus de père; et le jour n'est pas loin
Qui de ma mort encor doit le rendre témoin.
Déjà mille ennemis attaquent son enfance.
Vous seul pouvez contre eux embrasser sa défense.
Mais un secret remords agite mes esprits.
Je crains d'avoir fermé votre oreille à ses cris.
Je tremble que sur lui votre juste colère
Ne poursuive bientôt une odieuse mère.

HIPPOLYTE

Madame, je n'ai point des sentiments si bas.

PHÈDRE

Quand vous me haïrez, je ne m'en plaindrais pas,
Seigneur. Vous m'avez vue attachée à vous nuire;
Dans le fond de mon cœur vous ne pouviez pas lire.
A votre inimitié j'ai pris soin de m'offrir.
Aux bords que j'habitais je n'ai pu vous souffrir.
En public, en secret, contre vous déclarée,
J'ai voulu par des mers en être séparée.

78

SCENE 5

Phaedra, Hippolytus, Œnone

PHAEDRA

He's there. My blood runs back into my heart.
And I forget what I have come to say.

ŒNONE

Think of a son whose only hope you are.

PHAEDRA

I hear you leave us, Sir, in haste. I come
To add my tears to yours, and for my son
Plead my anxiety. No more has he
A father; and the day is not far off
Which will make him a witness to my death.
Already enemies innumerable
Are ready to attack his childhood state;
You are the only one who can embrace
His cause against them, and defend his youth.
But a concealed remorse gnaws at my heart:
I fear I may have shut your ears against
His cries. I tremble lest it be in him
Your righteous anger soon should persecute
His justly hated mother . . .

HIPPOLYTUS

Madam, I feel no sentiment so base.

PHAEDRA

If you should hate me, I would not complain,
Prince; you have seen me bent on hurting you.
But to the bottom of my heart you could not read.
I took great trouble to incur your hate.
I could not bear you to be near the shores
That I inhabit. I declared myself your foe,
In public and in private; longed for seas

79

J'ai même défendu, par une expresse loi,
Qu'on osât prononcer votre nom devant moi.
Si pourtant à l'offense on mesure la peine,
Si la haine peut seule attirer votre haine,
Jamais femme ne fut plus digne de pitié,
Et moins digne, Seigneur, de votre inimitié.

Des droits de ses enfants une mère jalouse
Pardonne rarement au fils d'une autre épouse.
Madame, je le sais. Les soupçons importuns
Sont d'un second hymen les fruits les plus communs.
Toute autre aurait pour moi pris les mêmes ombrages,
Et j'en aurais peut-être essuyé plus d'outrages.

Ah! Seigneur, que le ciel, j'ose ici l'attester,
De cette loi commune a voulu m'excepter!
Qu'un soin bien différent me trouble et me dévore!

Madame, il n'est pas temps de vous troubler encore.
Peut-être votre epoux voit encore le jour;
Le ciel peut à nos pleurs accorder son retour.
Neptune le protège, et ce Dieu tutélaire
Ne sera pas en vain imploré par mon père.

On ne voit point deux fois le rivage des morts,
Seigneur. Puisque Thésée a vu les sombres bords,
En vain vous espérez qu'un Dieu vous le renvoie;
Et l'avare Achéron ne lâche point sa proie.
Que dis-je? Il n'est point mort, puisqu'il respire en vous
Toujours devant mes yeux je crois voir mon époux.
Je le vois, je lui parle; et mon cœur. . . . Je m'égare,
Seigneur, ma folle ardeur malgré moi se déclare.

To separate us; even made a law
That none before me dare to speak your name.
And yet if punishment should be prescribed
To the offence, if only hatred drew
Your hatred in return, never was there
A woman so deserving pity, so
Little, from you, deserving enmity.

HIPPOLYTUS

A mother, jealous of her children's rights,
Seldom forgives the son of a first wife.
Nagging suspicions are the common fate
Of those who make a second marriage.
Anyone else would have resented me,
And might perhaps have made me suffer more.

PHAEDRA

Ah, Prince, how Heav'n has from that general law
Excepted me, be that same Heav'n my judge!
How different is the canker eating me.

HIPPOLYTUS

Madam, there is no need to vex yourself.
Perhaps your husband still beholds the light;
It may be Heav'n may grant him safe return
In answer to our tears. Neptune protects
My father as his tutelary God,
And will not be invoked by him in vain.

PHAEDRA

No one views twice the mansions of the dead.
No, no, my Lord, since once Theseus has seen
Those gloomy shores, in vain you hope some God
May send him back; for greedy Acheron
Does not release his prey. And yet, I think
He is not dead, but breathes in you. I see
My husband still before me—speak to him!
My heart—oh I am mad! Do what I will
I cannot hide my passion.

Je vois de votre amour l'effet prodigieux.
Tout mort qu'il est, Thésée est présent à vos yeux;
Toujours de son amour votre âme est embrasée.

PHÈDRE

Oui, Prince, je languis, je brûle pour Thésée.
Je l'aime, non point tel que l'ont vu les enfers,
Volage adorateur de mille objets divers,
Qui va du dieu des morts déshonorer la couche;
Mais fidèle, mais fier, et même un peu farouche,
Charmant, jeune, traînant tous les cœurs après soi,
Tel qu'on dépeint nos dieux, ou tel que je vous voi.
Il avait votre port, vos yeux, votre langage,
Cette noble pudeur colorait son visage,
Lorsque de notre Crète il traversa les flots,
Digne sujet des vœux des filles de Minos.
Que faisiez-vous alors? Pourquoi, sans Hippolyte,
Des héros de la Grèce assembla-t-il l'élite?
Pourquoi, trop jeune encor, ne pûtes-vous alors
Entrer dans le vaisseau qui le mit sur nos bords?
Par vous aurait péri le monstre de la Crète,
Malgré tous les détours de sa vaste retraite.
Pour en développer l'embarras incertain,
Ma sœur du fil fatal eût armé votre main.
Mais non, dans ce dessein je l'aurais devancée;
L'amour m'en eût d'abord inspiré la pensée.
C'est moi, prince, c'est moi, dont l'utile secours
Vous eût du Labyrinthe enseigné les détours.
Que de soins m'eût coûtés cette tête charmante!
Un fil n'eût point assez rassuré votre amante.
Compagne du péril qu'il vous fallait chercher,
Moi-même devant vous j'aurais voulu marcher;

Yes, I see
The palpable effect of your great love:
Theseus, though dead, is present to your eyes;
Your heart still smoulders with its love for him.

PHAEDRA

Yes, Prince, I languish and I long for Theseus.
I love him, but not as the Shades know him:
The inconstant lover of so many loves,
Who now would ravish even Pluto's bride!
But faithful, proud, even to a slight disdain;
Young, charming, drawing all hearts after him,
As Gods are painted. Or as I see you now,
He had your walk, your eyes, your way of speaking;
He could blush like you, when to the isle
Of Crete, my childhood's home, he crossed the waves,
Worthy to win the love of Minos' daughters.
What were you doing then? Why, without you
Did he assemble all the flower of Greece?
Oh why were you too young to have embarked
Within the ship that brought him to our shores?
You would have been the monster's killer then,
In spite of all the windings of his maze.
To find your way in that uncertain dark
My sister would have armed you with the thread.
But no! In this design I would have been
Ahead of her, my sister! Me, not her,
It would have been whom Love at first inspired;
And I it would have been, Prince, I, whose aid
Had taught you all the Labyrinth's crooked ways.
Oh, how I should have cared for this dear head!
A single thread would not have been enough
To satisfy your lover's fears for you.
I would myself have wished to lead the way,
And share the perils you were bound to face.
Phaedra, into the Labyrinth, with you

Et Phèdre au Labyrinthe avec vous descendue
Se serait avec vous retrouvée, ou perdue.

HIPPOLYTE

Dieux! qu'est-ce que j'entends? Madame, oubliez-vous
Que Thésée est mon père, et qu'il est votre époux?

PHÈDRE

Et sur quoi jugez-vous que j'en perds la mémoire,
Prince? Aurais-je perdu tout le soin de ma gloire?

HIPPOLYTE

Madame, pardonnez. J'avoue, en rougissant,
Que j'accusais à tort un discours innocent.
Ma honte ne peut plus soutenir votre vue;
Et je vais . . .

PHÈDRE

      Ah! cruel, tu m'as trop entendue.
Je t'en ai assez dit pour te tirer d'erreur.
Hé bien! connais donc Phèdre et toute sa fureur.
J'aime. Ne pense pas qu'au moment que je t'aime,
Innocente à mes yeux, je m'approuve moi-même,
Ni que du fol amour qui trouble ma raison
Ma lâche complaisance ait nourri le poison.
Objet infortuné des vengeances célestes,
Je m'abhorre encor plus que tu ne me détestes.
Les Dieux m'en sont témoins, ces Dieux qui dans mon flanc
Ont allumé le feu fatal à tout mon sang;
Ces Dieux qui se sont fait une gloire cruelle
De séduire le cœur d'une faible mortelle.
Toi-même en ton esprit rappelle le passé.
C'est peu de t'avoir fui, cruel, je t'ai chassé.
J'ai voulu te paraître odieuse, inhumaine;
Pour mieux te résister, j'ai recherché ta haine.
De quoi m'ont profité mes inutiles soins?
Tu me haïssais plus, je ne t'aimais pas moins.

84

Would have descended, and with you returned,
To safety, or with you have perished!

HIPPOLYTUS

　　　　　　　　　　　　Gods!
What is this that I hear? Have you forgotten
Theseus is my father and your husband?

PHAEDRA

Why should you think I have forgotten it?
Sir, do you think me careless of my honour?

HIPPOLYTUS

Forgive me, Madam. I confess I blush
To have misunderstood your innocent words.
I am too much ashamed to look at you.
I go . . .

PHAEDRA

　　　　Ah, cruel one! Too well, too well
You understand me. I have said enough
To save you from mistake. Well, look at me!
Know me, then—Phaedra—in my madness, know
I am in love. But do not dare to think
That I—in love with you—believe that I
Am innocent, or of myself approve.
Nor that the mad love now deranging me
Like poison in the blood, is fed at all
By cowardly connivance of my will.
Unlucky object of the spite of Gods,
I am not so detestable to you
As to myself. The Gods will bear me witness,
The same Gods who in my veins have poured
This burning fire, a doom to all my race;
The Gods who take a barbarous delight
In leading a poor mortal's heart astray!
Do you, yourself, recall to mind the past!
I did not only fly, I hounded you;

Tes malheurs te prêtaient encor de nouveaux charmes.
J'ai langui, j'ai séché, dans les feux, dans les larmes.
Il suffit de tes yeux pour t'en persuader,
Si tes yeux un moment pouvaient me regarder.
Que dis-je? Cet aveu que je te viens de faire,
Cet aveu si honteux, le crois-tu volontaire?
Tremblante pour un fils que je n'osais trahir,
Je te venais prier de ne le point haïr.
Faibles projets d'un cœur trop plein de ce qu'il aime!
Hélas! je ne t'ai pu parler que de toi-même.
Venge-toi, punis-moi d'un odieux amour.
Digne fils du héros qui t'a donné le jour,
Délivre l'univers d'un monstre qui t'irrite.
La veuve de Thésée ose aimer Hippolyte!
Crois-moi, ce monstre affreux ne doit point t'échapper.
Voilà mon cœur. C'est là que ta main doit frapper.
Impatient déjà d'expier son offense,
Au-devant de ton bras je le sens qui s'avance.
Frappe. Ou si tu le crois indigne de tes coups,
Si ta haine m'envie un supplice si doux,
Ou si d'un sang trop vil ta main serait trempée,
Au défaut de ton bras prête-moi ton épée.
Donne.

ŒNONE

Que faites-vous, Madame? Justes Dieux!
Mais on vient. Évitez des témoins odieux;
Venez, rentrez, fuyez une honte certaine.

I wanted you to think me odious,
I sought to appear inhuman in your eyes.
The better to resist your charm I sought
To make you hate me. Oh, what useless care!
You hated more. I loved you none the less.
Misfortunes only lent you added charm.
I have been drowned in tears, and scorched with fire.
Your own eyes might convince you of the truth,
If for one moment you could look at me.
What have I said? Can you believe that this
Confession I have just made to you—this
So shameful declaration I have made
Is voluntary? Can you think so? Ah!
Trembling in fear for safety of a son
Whom I dare not betray, I came to beg
You not to hate him. What a feeble plan
For any heart so full of what it loves.
I could speak to you only of yourself!
Oh take your vengeance, do, and punish me
For such a hideous and illicit love!
Your father was a hero, be like him,
And rid the world of one more monster now.
Does Theseus' widow dare to love his son?
Believe me you should not let her escape.
Here is my heart. Here, where your hand should strike,
It waits impatient to expiate
Its guilt. It leaps to meet your arm. Oh strike!
Or if your hatred envy me a blow
Of such sweet torture, or if blood too vile
You think would therefore drench your hand, then give,
Give me, if not your arm, at least your sword!
Give.

ŒNONE

Madam, what are you about? Oh Gods!
There's someone coming. You must not be seen.
Escape from certain shame. Come—come within.

87

SCÈNE 6

Hippolyte, Théramène

THÉRAMÈNE

Est-ce Phèdre qui fuit, ou plutôt qu'on entraîne?
Pourquoi, Seigneur, pourquoi ces marques de douleur?
Je vous vois sans épée, interdit, sans couleur?

HIPPOLYTE

Théramène, fuyons. Ma surprise est extrême.
Je ne puis sans horreur me regarder moi-même.
Phèdre . . . Mais non, grands Dieux! qu'en un profond
    oubli
Cet horrible secret demeure enseveli.

THÉRAMÈNE

Si vous voulez partir, la voile est préparée.
Mais Athènes, Seigneur, s'est déjà déclarée.
Ses chefs ont pris les voix de toutes ses tribus.
Votre frère l'emporte, et Phèdre a le dessus.

HIPPOLYTE

Phèdre?

THÉRAMÈNE

       Un héraut chargé des volontés d'Athènes
De l'État en ses mains vient remettre les rênes.
Son fils est roi, Seigneur.

HIPPOLYTE

           Dieux, qui la connaissez,
Est-ce donc sa vertu que vous récompensez?

THÉRAMÈNE

Cependant un bruit sourd veut que le Roi respire.
On prétend que Thésée a paru dans l'Épire.
Mais moi qui l'y cherchai, Seigneur, je sais trop bien . . .

SCENE 6

Hippolytus, Theramenes

THERAMENES

Is that Phaedra in flight? Or rather dragged
By someone off? What mean these signs of grief?
I see you without colour, sword, or speech . . .

HIPPOLYTUS

Let us fly, Theramenes! Extreme
Surprise confounds me. I can look
No more except with horror on myself.
Phaedra . . . But no, great Gods! Let this be kept
This horrible secret for ever dark.

THERAMENES

The ship is ready if you wish to sail.
But Athens has declared herself. Her chiefs
Already have the votes of all her tribes;
Your brother is elected. Phaedra wins.

HIPPOLYTUS

Phaedra?

THERAMENES

          A herald charged with Athens' will
Has just arrived to place within her hands
The reins of power. Her son is King, my Lord.

HIPPOLYTUS

Ye Gods, who know her! Is it virtue, Gods!
Her virtue that you recompense like this?

THERAMENES

But rumour has it that the King's alive;
That in Epirus, Theseus has been seen.
But I who searched there know too well my Lord . . .

N'importe, écoutons tout, et ne négligeons rien.
Examinons ce bruit, remontons à sa source:
S'il ne mérite pas d'interrompre ma course,
Partons; et quelque prix qu'il en puisse coûter,
Mettons le sceptre aux mains dignes de le porter.

No matter. Let us hear all and neglect
Nothing. This rumour must be traced at once
Back to its source, examined; if it be
Found insufficient to delay my flight
Let us set sail, and cost what price it may
Place in deserving hands the sceptre's sway.

ACTE III

Phèdre, Œnone

PHÈDRE

Ah! que l'on porte ailleurs les honneurs qu'on m'envoie.
Importune, peux-tu souhaiter qu'on me voie?
De quoi viens-tu flatter mon esprit désolé?
Cache-moi bien plutôt: je n'ai que trop parlé.
Mes fureurs au dehors ont osé se répandre.
J'ai dit ce que jamais on ne devait entendre.
Ciel! comme il m'écoutait! Par combien de détours
L'insensible a longtemps éludé mes discours!
Comme il ne respirait qu'une retraite prompte!
Et combien sa rougeur a redoublé ma honte!
Pourquoi détournais-tu mon funeste dessein?
Hélas! quand son épée allait chercher mon sein,
A-t-il pâli pour moi? me l'a-t-il arrachée?
Il suffit que ma main l'ait une fois touchée,
Je l'ai rendue horrible à ses yeux inhumains;
Et ce fer malheureux profanerait ses mains.

ŒNONE

Ainsi, dans vos malheurs ne songeant qu'à vous plaindre,
Vous nourrissez un feu qu'il vous faudrait éteindre.
Ne vaudrait-il pas mieux, digne sang de Minos,
Dans de plus nobles soins chercher votre repos,
Contre un ingrat qui plaît recourir à la fuite,
Régner, et de l'État embrasser la conduite?

ACT III

SCENE I

Phaedra, Œnone

PHAEDRA

Ah, let them take elsewhere the honours sent
To me. Stop driving me. Can you desire
That anyone should see me as I am?
With what are you attempting to console
My desolation? Rather try to hide me.
I have said too much. My madness has burst out.
I have said things which never should be heard.
Oh Heavens, how he listened! How he tried
To wriggle out of seeing what I meant.
How he was sniffing for a quick escape!
And how his blushes made me sink in shame.
Why did you turn me from the death I sought?
Ah, when his sword was almost in my breast,
Did he grow pale in fear for me? Or try
To snatch it from me? No, it was enough:
My miserable hand had touched his sword
And rendered it for ever horrible
In his inhuman eyes; and that unhappy blade
Is now profaned for ever.

ŒNONE

                          Brooding so
Complaining of your griefs, you only fan
A fire whose flames you must at once put out.
Would it not be more worthy of the blood
Of Minos to find peace in nobler cares?
Resort to flight from such a wretch's charm,
Embrace the conduct of the State, and reign⸩

Moi, régner! Moi, ranger un Etat sous ma loi,
Quand ma faible raison ne règne plus sur moi!
Lorsque j'ai de mes sens abandonné l'empire!
Quand sous un joug honteux à peine je respire!
Quand je me meurs!

ŒNONE

Fuyez.

PHÈDRE

Je ne le puis quitter.

ŒNONE

Vous l'osâtes bannir, vous n'osez l'éviter.

PHÈDRE

Il n'est plus temps. Il sait mes ardeurs insensées.
De l'austère pudeur les bornes sont passées.
J'ai déclaré ma honte aux yeux de mon vainqueur,
Et l'espoir, malgré moi, s'est glissé dans mon cœur.
Toi-même, rappelant ma force défaillante,
Et mon âme déjà sur mes lèvres errante,
Par tes conseils flatteurs tu m'as su ranimer.
Tu m'as fait entrevoir que je pouvais l'aimer.

ŒNONE

Hélas! de vos malheurs innocente ou coupable,
De quoi pour vous sauver n'étais-je point capable?
Mais si jamais l'offense irrita vos esprits,
Pouvez-vous d'un superbe oublier les mépris?

PHAEDRA

I reign? Shall I, shall I make laws of state
When my poor reason reigns no more on me?
When I have lost the empire of my senses?
When I, so choked by shame, can scarcely breathe?
When I am dying.

ŒNONE

Fly.

PHAEDRA

I cannot leave him.

ŒNONE

You dared to banish him; why dare you not
Avoid him?

PHAEDRA

Oh, the time for that is past.
He knows, I let him see, the full extent
Of my insane desires. The boundaries
Of modesty, austerity, are passed.
I have declared my shame before the eyes
Of him, my conqueror. Against my will
Hope stole into my heart. And you it was,
You, who with flattering advice revived
My failing strength, recalled my errant soul
When it was floating past my lips. And you
Who made me think that I *might* love him—you.

ŒNONE

Alas! Whether I be to blame or not
For your misfortunes, what is there on earth
Of which I am not capable to save you?
But if your spirits ever were aroused
To fire by insult, can you so endure,
Forget and pardon the contempt of one
So hideously proud? With what a look,

Avec quels yeux cruels sa rigueur obstinée
Vous laissait à ses pieds peu s'en faut prosternée!
Que son farouche orgueil le rendait odieux!
Que Phèdre en ce moment n'avait-elle mes yeux?

PHÈDRE

Œnone, il peut quitter cet orgueil qui te blesse.
Nourri dans les forêts, il en a la rudesse.
Hippolyte, endurci par de sauvages lois,
Entend parler d'amour pour la première fois.
Peut-être sa surprise a causé son silence,
Et nos plaintes peut-être ont trop de violence.

ŒNONE

Songez qu'une barbare en son sein l'a formé.

PHÈDRE

Quoique Scythe et barbare, elle a pourtant aimé.

ŒNONE

Il a pour tout le sexe une haine fatale.

PHÈDRE

Je ne me verrai point préférer de rivale.
Enfin tous tes conseils ne sont plus de saison.
Sers ma fureur, Œnone, et non point ma raison.
Il oppose à l'amour un cœur inaccessible:
Cherchons pour l'attaquer quelque endroit plus sensible.
Les charmes d'un empire ont paru le toucher;
Athènes l'attirait, il n'a pu s'en cacher;
Déjà de ses vaisseaux la pointe était tournée,
Et la voile flottait aux vents abandonnée.

With what indifferent, cruel eyes he watched
You at his—almost prostrate at his feet!
How hateful then his savage pride appeared.
Why did you not then see him with my eyes?

PHAEDRA

Œnone, it could be that he could doff
This pride which so offends you. Bred
In forests wild, he has their uncouth ways;
And, hardened by their savage laws, perhaps
He now hears talk of love for the first time!
Perhaps it is surprise that silenced him—
And our complaints—perhaps too violent?

ŒNONE

Do not forget a savage gave him birth.

PHAEDRA

Oh, Scythian and barbarian, at least
She knew what love was!

ŒNONE

He does not. You know
That for our sex he has a hatred fierce,
A famed aversion.

PHAEDRA

Then I shall not see
A rival in his heart preferred to me!
But anyway your counsels come too late.
Oh serve my madness, dear Œnone, not
My reason. Is he inaccessible
To love? Then let us seek to find a place
More vulnerable to attack. The charms
Of empire seemed to touch a chord in him:
That Athens drew him he could not conceal.
His vessels' prows were pointed there: the sails
Were set; the breeze is in them now! You, go

Va trouver de ma part ce jeune ambitieux,
Œnone; fais briller la couronne à ses yeux.
Qu'il mette sur son front le sacré diadème;
Je ne veux que l'honneur de l'attacher moi-même.
Cédons-lui ce pouvoir que je ne puis garder.
Il instruira mon fils dans l'art de commander;
Peut-être il voudra bien lui tenir lieu de père.
Je mets sous son pouvoir et le fils et la mère.
Pour le fléchir enfin tente tous les moyens:
Tes discours trouveront plus d'accès que les miens.
Presse, pleure, gémis; plains-lui Phèdre mourante;
Ne rougis point de prendre une voix suppliante.
Je t'avoûrai de tout; je n'espère qu'en toi.
Va: j'attends ton retour pour disposer de moi.

SCÈNE 2

Phèdre, seule

O toi, qui vois la honte où je suis descendue,
Implacable Vénus, suis-je assez confondue?
Tu ne saurais plus loin pousser ta cruauté.
Ton triomphe est parfait; tous tes traits ont porté.
Cruelle, si tu veux une gloire nouvelle,
Attaque un ennemi qui te soit plus rebelle.
Hippolyte te fuit; et bravant ton courroux,
Jamais à tes autels n'a fléchi les genoux.
Ton nom semble offenser ses superbes oreilles.
Déesse, venge-toi: nos causes sont pareilles.
Qu'il aime. . . . Mais déjà tu reviens sur tes pas,
Œnone? On me déteste, on ne t'écoute pas.

Find this ambitious boy and speak to him
For me: dangle the crown before his eyes.
Let him assume the sacred diadem,
I only ask the joy of placing it
There on his brow. Let him accept this power
I cannot keep, and he shall teach my son
How to rule men. It may be he will deign
To be a father to him. Son and mother
He shall control. Try every means to move him.
Your words will find more favour than can mine.
Cry, groan, and weep! Show Phaedra dying;
Be not ashamed to plead and supplicate
You are my only hope. I will approve
All you can say, and wait for your return
To know what shall become of Phaedra—go.

SCENE 2

Phaedra, alone

Implacable Venus, oh Thou who seest
To what a depth of shame I am brought low,
Am I not low enough? No further stretch
Thy cruelty. Thy shafts have all gone home
And Thou hast triumphed! Wouldst Thou win a new
Renown? Attack a heart more obdurate!
Hippolytus escapes Thee, braves Thy wrath,
And never at Thy altar bowed his knees.
Thy name is an offence to his proud ears
It seems. Goddess, our interests are the same!
Avenge Thyself! Make him love me . . . But what?
Œnone back already? He detests
Me then? He would not even listen to . . .

SCÈNE 3

Phèdre, Œnone

ŒNONE

Il faut d'un vain amour étouffer la pensée,
Madame. Rappelez votre vertu passée.
Le Roi, qu'on a cru mort, va paraître à vos yeux;
Thésée est arrivé, Thésée est dans ces lieux.
Le peuple, pour le voir, court et se précipite.
Je sortais par votre ordre, et cherchais Hippolyte,
Lorsque jusques au ciel mille cris élancés . . .

PHÈDRE

Mon époux est vivant, Œnone, c'est assez.
J'ai fait l'indigne aveu d'un amour qui l'outrage.
Il vit: je ne veux pas en savoir davantage.

ŒNONE

Quoi?

PHÈDRE

Je te l'ai prédit; mais tu n'as pas voulu.
Sur mes justes remords tes pleurs ont prévalu.
Je mourais ce matin digne d'être pleurée;
J'ai suivi tes conseils, je meurs déshonorée.

ŒNONE

Vous mourez?

PHÈDRE

Juste ciel! qu'ai-je fait aujourd'hui?
Mon époux va paraître et son fils avec lui.

SCENE 3

Phaedra, Œnone

ŒNONE

Madam, you must at all costs suffocate
The very thought of such a useless love.
Recall the virtue that you once possessed.
The King, who was thought dead, will soon appear
Before your eyes! Theseus is in this place!
Theseus is here! The people flock to see him.
I went, by your command, to find the Prince,
Hippolytus, when up into the skies
I heard a thousand shouts go rocketing . . .

PHAEDRA

My husband is alive! That is enough.
Œnone I have owned—confessed—a love
Which is to him an outrage! He still lives!
I cannot hear another word.

ŒNONE

But what . . .

PHAEDRA

I told you so! This I foretold! But you
Refused to hear. Over my just remorse
Your tears prevailed. Alas, if I had died
This morning I had died at least, at least
Deserving pity. Your advice I took
And now I die dishonoured.

ŒNONE

Die?

PHAEDRA

Oh Gods,
What have I done this day? My husband comes,

Je verrai le témoin de ma flamme adultère
Observer de quel front j'ose aborder son père,
Le cœur gros de soupirs, qu'il n'a point écoutés,
L'œil humide de pleurs, par l'ingrat rebutés.
Penses-tu que sensible à l'honneur de Thésée,
Il lui cache l'ardeur dont je suis embrasée?
Laissera-t-il trahir et son père et son roi?
Pourra-t-il contenir l'horreur qu'il a pour moi?
Il se tairait en vain. Je sais mes perfidies,
Œnone, et ne suis point de ces femmes hardies
Qui, goûtant dans le crime une tranquille paix,
Ont su se faire un front qui ne rougit jamais.
Je connais mes fureurs, je les rappelle toutes.
Il me semble déjà que ces murs, que ces voûtes
Vont prendre la parole, et prêts à m'accuser,
Attendent mon époux pour le désabuser.
Mourons. De tant d'horreurs qu'un trépas me délivre.
Est-ce un malheur si grand que de cesser de vivre?
La mort aux malheureux ne cause point d'effroi.
Je ne crains que le nom que je laisse après moi.
Pour mes tristes enfants quel affreux héritage!
Le sang de Jupiter doit enfler leur courage;
Mais quelque juste orgueil qu'inspire un sang si beau,
Le crime d'une mère est un pesant fardeau.
Je tremble qu'un discours, hélas! trop véritable,
Un jour ne leur reproche une mère coupable.
Je tremble qu'opprimés de ce poids odieux
L'un ni l'autre jamais n'ose lever les yeux.

ŒNONE

Il n'en faut point douter, je les plains l'un et l'autre;
Jamais crainte ne fut plus juste que la vôtre.

With him, his son; and I shall see the witness
Of my adulterous love watch with what face
I greet his father: with my heart still big
With passion he refused; my eyes still wet
With tears that could not move him. Do you think
That for his father's sake he will
Conceal the fire he knows consuming me?
Let me betray his father and his King?
Will he be able to keep back the horror
He has for me? His silence would be vain.
I know my treason. Œnone, I am not
One of those hardened women who can taste
Tranquillity in crime, and show a brow
Unblushing, unashamed. I recognize
My madness. I recall it all. I think
These walls, this vaulted roof can speak, and will,
At any moment, will take up the tale:
They, ready to accuse me, only wait
My husband's presence to reveal my shame.
I am resolved to die, for death alone
From all this horror can deliver me.
Is it so great calamity to die?
Death is not feared by those in misery.
I only fear the name I leave behind.
For my unhappy sons a hideous
Inheritance. The blood of Jupiter
Is in their veins and should keep up their hearts;
But even to so great a pride of race
A mother's guilt will be a heavy load.
I am afraid of that reproach one day,
Only too true a tale, laid to their charge.
I am afraid that, crushed beneath the weight
Of such a millstone, they will never dare
Lift up their eyes.

ŒNONE

Of course I pity both.
Never was fear more real than yours. Why then

Mais à de tels affronts pourquoi les exposer?
Pourquoi contre vous-même allez-vous déposer?
C'en est fait: on dira que Phèdre, trop coupable,
De son époux trahi fuit l'aspect redoutable.
Hippolyte est heureux qu'aux dépens de vos jours
Vous-même en expirant appuyiez ses discours.
A votre accusateur que pourrai-je répondre?
Je serai devant lui trop facile à confondre.
De son triomphe affreux je le verrai jouir,
Et conter votre honte à qui voudra l'ouïr.
Ah! que plutôt du ciel la flamme me dévore!
Mais ne me trompez point, vous est-il cher encore?
De quel œil voyez-vous ce prince audacieux?

PHÈDRE

Je le vois comme un monstre effroyable à mes yeux.

ŒNONE

Pourquoi donc lui céder une victoire entière?
Vous le craignez. Osez l'accuser la première
Du crime dont il peut vous charger aujourd'hui.
Qui vous démentira? Tout parle contre lui:
Son épée en vos mains heureusement laissée,
Votre trouble présent, votre douleur passée,
Son père par vos cris dès longtemps prévenu,
Et déjà son exil par vous-même obtenu.

PHÈDRE

Moi, que j'ose opprimer et noircir l'innocence?

ŒNONE

Mon zèle n'a besoin que de votre silence.

Expose them to such insults? Why accuse
Yourself? All's over then. It will be said
That Phaedra, conscious of her guilt, has fled
From her wronged husband's fearful countenance.
Hippolytus will be rejoiced to find
That by your death you lend his charge support.
What could I answer your accuser? What?
I should be far too easily confused;
And I should have to watch his horrible
Success, and hear him tell to every ear
The story of your shame. Rather than that,
May fire from Heaven devour me! Tell me true,
Without deceit, do you still love this Prince?
How does his proud contempt of you appear
Now in your eyes?

PHAEDRA

                    Alas, I look on him
As on a monster, frightful to my sight.

ŒNONE

Why then surrender him the victory?
You fear him. Then be bold, accuse him first!
Charge him with the same crime of which today
He can accuse you! Who can call you liar?
All counts against him. His sword, in your hands
Luckily left, your present state of mind;
Your former trouble and repeated cries
Of warning to his father long ago;
Even his exile it was you obtained!

PHAEDRA

And would you have me bear false witness? Me?

ŒNONE

I would have you do nothing but keep quiet!
My passionate devotion to you needs
Nothing from you but silence. I, like you,

Tremblante comme vous, j'en sens quelque remords.
Vous me verriez plus prompte affronter mille morts.
Mais puisque je vous perds sans ce triste remède,
Votre vie est pour moi d'un prix à qui tout cède.
Je parlerai. Thésée, aigri par mes avis,
Bornera sa vengeance à l'exil de son fils.
Un père, et punissant, Madame, est toujours père:
Un supplice léger suffit à sa colère.
Mais le sang innocent dût-il être versé,
Que ne demande point votre honneur menacé?
C'est un trésor trop cher pour oser le commettre.
Quelque loi qu'il vous dicte, il faut vous y soumettre,
Madame; et pour sauver votre honneur combattu,
Il faut immoler tout, et même la vertu.
On vient; je vois Thésée.

PHÈDRE

           Ah! je vois Hippolyte;
Dans ses yeux insolents je vois ma perte écrite.
Fais ce que tu voudras, je m'abandonne à toi.
Dans le trouble où je suis, je ne puis rien pour moi.

SCÈNE 4

Thésée, Hippolyte, Phèdre, Œnone, Théramène

THÉSÉE

La fortune à mes vœux cesse d'être opposée,
Madame, et dans vos bras met . . .

PHÈDRE

                 Arrêtez, Thésée,
Et ne profanez point des transports si charmants.
Je ne mérite plus ces doux empressements.

Am trembling, and indeed I feel remorse.
You'd see, I'd rather face a thousand deaths:
But since, without this bitter remedy,
I'd lose you, and to me your life outweighs
All else, I'll speak! Theseus, even enraged,
Will do no worse than banish him again.
A father, when he punishes, remains
A father still. His wrath will be content
With a light penalty. But if it must
Be guiltless blood that's made to flow, why should
Your threatened honour stop at that? You know
It is a treasure far too dear to risk.
Whatever it dictates, for you is law.
For reputation's sake you must submit.
To save your honour you must sacrifice
All, even conscience! Someone comes; I see
Theseus.

PHAEDRA

And I, Hippolytus. I see
In his cold eyes my ruin written large.
Do what you will, I leave myself to you.
I am in such a whirlpool of distress
That for myself I can do nothing more.

SCENE 4

Theseus, Hippolytus, Phaedra, Œnone, Theramenes

THESEUS

Fortune, so long against me, now relents,
And to your arms, my dearest love, restores . . .

PHAEDRA

Stop, Theseus, stop! Do not profane the words
Of such a gentle greeting, due no more
To me, unworthy now to hear them. You

Vous êtes offensé. La fortune jalouse
N'a pas en votre absence épargné votre épouse.
Indigne de vous plaire et de vous approcher,
Je ne dois désormais songer qu'à me cacher.

SCÈNE 5

Thésée, Hippolyte, Théramène

THÉSÉE

Quel est l'étrange accueil qu'on fait à votre père,
Mon fils?

HIPPOLYTE

         Phèdre peut seule expliquer ce mystère.
Mais si mes vœux ardents vous peuvent émouvoir,
Permettez-moi, Seigneur, de ne la plus revoir.
Souffrez que pour jamais le tremblant Hippolyte
Disparaisse des lieux que votre épouse habite.

THÉSÉE

Vous, mon fils, me quitter?

HIPPOLYTE

              Je ne la cherchais pas:
C'est vous qui sur ces bords conduisîtes ses pas.
Vous daignâtes, Seigneur, aux rives de Trézène
Confier en partant Aricie et la Reine.
Je fus même chargé du soin de les garder.
Mais quels soins désormais peuvent me retarder?
Assez dans les forêts mon oisive jeunesse
Sur de vils ennemis a montré son adresse.
Ne pourrai-je, en fuyant un indigne repos,
D'un sang plus glorieux teindre mes javelots?
Vous n'aviez pas encore atteint l'âge où je touche,
Déjà plus d'un tyran, plus d'un monstre farouche

108

Have been, in absence, wronged. Malicious fate
Has chosen not to spare your wife. Unfit
To please—or even to approach you now—
I must seek only where to hide myself.

SCENE 5

Theseus, Hippolytus, Theramenes

THESEUS

What is the meaning of this welcome, son?
A strange one for a father.

HIPPOLYTUS

        Only she,
Phaedra, can solve this mystery. But if
My heart's desire can move you, give me leave
Never to see her more. Let me, my Lord,
Trembling Hippolytus escape for ever
Any place inhabited by her.

THESEUS

You, my son, going?

HIPPOLYTUS

        I did not seek her, Sir!
It was yourself who led her to these shores.
Departing, you thought fit, my Lord, to trust
Aricia and the Queen to this Trozene,
And I was left their guardian. But now
Such cares no longer need to keep me here.
My lazy youthful power has shown enough
Its skill in conquering paltry game
In forests hereabout. May I not leave
Inglorious ease, and dip my javelin
In nobler blood? You were not yet my age
When more than one fierce monster, more than one

109

Avait de votre bras senti la pesanteur;
Déjà, de l'insolence heureux persécuteur,
Vous aviez des deux mers assuré les rivages.
Le libre voyageur ne craignait plus d'outrages;
Hercule, respirant sur le bruit de vos coups,
Déjà de son travail se reposait sur vous.
Et moi, fils inconnu d'un si glorieux père,
Je suis même encor loin des traces de ma mère.
Souffrez que mon courage ose enfin s'occuper.
Souffrez, si quelque monstre a pu vous échapper,
Que j'apporte à vos pieds sa dépouille honorable,
Ou que d'un beau trépas la mémoire durable,
Éternisant des jours si noblement finis,
Prouve à tout l'univers que j'étais votre fils.

THÉSÉE

Que vois-je? Quelle horreur dans ces lieux répandue
Fait fuir devant mes yeux ma famille éperdue?
Si je reviens si craint et si peu désiré,
O ciel, de ma prison pourquoi m'as-tu tiré?
Je n'avais qu'un ami. Son imprudente flamme
Du tyran de l'Épire allait ravir la femme;
Je servais à regret ses desseins amoureux;
Mais le sort irrité nous aveuglait tous deux.
Le tyran m'a surpris sans défense et sans armes.
J'ai vu Pirithoüs, triste objet de mes larmes,
Livré par ce barbare à des monstres cruels
Qu'il nourrissait du sang des malheureux mortels.
Moi-même, il m'enferma dans des cavernes sombres,
Lieux profonds, et voisins de l'empire des ombres.
Les Dieux, après six mois, enfin m'ont regardé:
J'ai su tromper les yeux de qui j'étais gardé.
D'un perfide ennemi j'ai purgé la nature;

Tyrant had felt the weight of your strong **arm.**
Already happily renowned as scourge
Of villainy, you had along the shores
Of both the Seas made peace. The travellers
Feared piracy no more; and Hercules
Himself, hearing of your exploits, relied
On you, and rested from his toils. While **I,**
Unknown son of so brave a father, lag
Behind even my mother's fame. Oh let
My courage have employment. And if still
Some monster has escaped you, let me lay
The glorious spoils down at your feet, or let
The lasting memory of a noble death
Immortalize my honourable end,
And prove to all the world I was your son.

THESEUS

Why what is this? What horror in this place
Makes fly my terror-stricken family?
If I return to find myself so fear'd,
So little welcome, why, Oh Heav'n, did you
Release me from my prison? My one friend,
Ruled by misguided passion, sought to steal
The wife of the dictator of Epirus.
I helped the lover—I regret to say;
But bad luck made us blind, the two of us:
The tyrant took me by surprise, unarmed,
Defenceless. Pirithoüs, my poor friend,
The piteous object of my futile tears,
I watched by this barbarian's orders flung
To ravening savage beasts by him kept fed
On miserable human blood. Myself
He shut up in the bowels of the earth,
A dungeon deep enough to reach the edge
Of the dark Underworld. The Gods at last
After six months, inclined a look my way,
And I was able to deceive my guards.
I purged the world of that foul enemy

A ses monstres lui-même a servi de pâture.
Et lorsque avec transport je pense m'approcher
De tout ce que les Dieux m'ont laissé de plus cher;
Que dis-je? quand mon âme, à soi-même rendue,
Vient se rassasier d'une si chère vue,
Je n'ai pour tout accueil que des frémissements:
Tout fuit, tout se refuse à mes embrassements.
Et moi-même, éprouvant la terreur que j'inspire,
Je voudrais être encore dans les prisons d'Épire.
Parlez. Phèdre se plaint que je suis outragé.
Qui m'a trahi? Pourquoi ne suis-je pas vengé?
La Grèce, à qui mon bras fut tant de fois utile,
A-t-elle au criminel accordé quelque asile?
Vous ne répondez point. Mon fils, mon propre fils
Est-il d'intelligence avec mes ennemis?
Entrons. C'est trop garder un doute qui m'accable.
Connaissons à la fois le crime et le coupable.
Que Phèdre explique enfin le trouble où je la voi.

SCÈNE 6

Hippolyte, Théramène

HIPPOLYTE

Où tendait ce discours qui m'a glacé d'effroi?
Phèdre, toujours en proie à sa fureur extrême,
Veut-elle s'accuser et se perdre elle-même?
Dieux! que dira le Roi? Quel funeste poison
L'amour a répandu sur toute sa maison!
Moi-même, plein d'un feu que sa haine réprouve,
Quel il m'a vu jadis, et quel il me retrouve!
De noirs pressentiments viennent m'épouvanter.

And served him up as fodder to his beasts.
But when, with joy exulting, I approach
All that the Gods have left to me most dear,
And when—what am I saying?—When, my soul
But just restored to life and to itself—
I come to feast upon so dear a sight
My welcome is a shudder. All take flight.
All run away from my embrace. Myself,
Infected with the terror I inspire,
I wish a prisoner still in Epirus!
Phaedra complains that I have suffered wrong.
Who has betrayed me? Speak! Has Greece to whom
My strength has been of use so many times
Afforded shelter to the criminal?
You do not answer. Is my son, my own
Dear son confederate with my enemies?
Let us go in. My mind is overwhelmed
With sickening doubt, and I must know at once
What is the crime, and who the criminal.
Let Phaedra tell, let her explain at least
The state in which I found her. I must know.

SCENE 6

Hippolytus, Theramenes

HIPPOLYTUS

What was he driving at with words which freeze
My blood with fear? Will Phaedra, still the prey
To such a furious fever, seek at once
To accuse and so condemn herself? Oh Gods!
What will the King say? What a fatal dole
Of poison Love has spread on all his house!
Myself so deep in love of which his hate
Must disapprove. Oh, how did I appear
Once in his eyes—and how I now appear!
Such black forebodings terrify my soul.

113

Mais l'innocence enfin n'a rien à redouter.
Allons, cherchons ailleurs par quelle heureuse adresse
Je pourrai de mon père émouvoir la tendresse,
Et lui dire un amour qu'il peut vouloir troubler,
Mais que tout son pouvoir ne saurait ébranler.

But surely innocence need never fear?
Come, let us seek some happy speech to move
My father's sympathy towards my love,
Which he may wish to cross, but which, I stake,
Not all his power will avail to shake.

ACTE IV

SCÈNE I

Thésée, Œnone

THÉSÉE

Ah! qu'est-ce que j'entends? Un traître, un téméraire
Préparait cet outrage à l'honneur de son père?
Avec quelle rigueur, destin, tu me poursuis!
Je ne sais où je vais, je ne sais où je suis.
O tendresse! ô bonté trop mal récompensée!
Projet audacieux! détestable pensée!
Pour parvenir au but de ses noires amours,
L'insolent de la force empruntait le secours.
J'ai reconnu le fer, instrument de sa rage,
Ce fer dont je l'armai pour un plus noble usage.
Tous les liens du sang n'ont pu le retenir?
Et Phèdre différait à le faire punir?
Le silence de Phèdre épargnait le coupable?

ŒNONE

Phèdre épargnait plutôt un père déplorable.
Honteuse du dessein d'un amant furieux
Et du feu criminel qu'il a pris dans ses yeux,
Phèdre mourait, Seigneur, et sa main meurtrière
Éteignait de ses yeux l'innocente lumière.
J'ai vu lever le bras, j'ai couru la sauver.
Moi seule à votre amour j'ai su la conserver;
Et plaignant à la fois son trouble et vos alarmes,
J'ai servi, malgré moi, d'interprète à ses larmes.

ACT IV

SCENE I

Theseus, Œnone

THESEUS

Ah! What is this I hear? Presumptuous
Foolhardy traitor! Could he so disgrace
His father's honour? How relentlessly
Oh Destiny, Thou dost pursue me still.
I know not where I go—nor where I am.
Oh, kindness and affection ill repaid!
Shameless attempt! Abominable thought!
He even had the insolence to use
Force to achieve his foul desires. I know
This sword which served him in his rage, this sword
With which I armed him for a nobler use.
Could not the ties of blood restrain his lust?
And Phaedra,—slow to have him punish'd! Why?
Her silence was to spare the culprit? Yes?

ŒNONE

Rather to spare the pitiable father.
That she should have inspired a love so mad,
That she should be the object of his lust,
So shamed her that she would have died, my Lord.
By her own murderous hand the innocent
Light was to be extinguished from her eyes.
I saw her raise her arm. I ran to help.
Alone I saved her for your Majesty.
And, pitying her fear and your alarm, I have,
Against my will, interpreted her tears.

THÉSÉE

Le perfide! Il n'a pu s'empêcher de pâlir.
De crainte, en l'abordant, je l'ai vu tressaillir.
Je me suis étonné de son peu d'allégresse;
Ses froids embrassements ont glacé ma tendresse.
Mais ce coupable amour dont il est dévoré
Dans Athènes déjà s'était-il déclaré?

ŒNONE

Seigneur, souvenez-vous des plaintes de la Reine.
Un amour criminel causa toute sa haine.

THÉSÉE

Et ce feu dans Trézène a donc recommencé?

ŒNONE

Je vous ai dit, Seigneur, tout ce qui s'est passé.
C'est trop laisser la Reine à sa douleur mortelle;
Souffrez que je vous quitte et me range auprès d'elle.

SCÈNE 2

Thésée, Hippolyte

THÉSÉE

Ah! le voici. Grands Dieux! à ce noble maintien
Quel œil ne serait pas trompé comme le mien?
Faut-il que sur le front d'un profane adultère
Brille de la vertu le sacré caractère?
Et ne devrait-on pas à des signes certains
Reconnaître le cœur des perfides humains?

THESEUS

What treachery! No wonder he turned pale.
I saw him flinch with fear when we first met.
I was surprised he showed so little joy.
His chill embraces froze my tenderness.
But was this guilty love devouring him,
Was it declared already? Was it known
In Athens?

ŒNONE

How the Queen complained, my Lord,
Do call to mind. It was forbidden love
That caused her hatred.

THESEUS

Then this fire broke out
Again at Trozene? Was that it?

ŒNONE

My Lord,
I've told you all. It's more than I can bear
To leave the Queen alone in mortal grief.
Permit me to withdraw and go to her.

SCENE 2

Theseus, Hippolytus

THESEUS

Ah, there he is! What eyes, great Gods, might not,
Like mine be fool'd by such a noble look?
Must virtue's sacred stamp shine on the brow
Of a profane adulterer? Oh why
Can we not recognize by certain signs
The black heart of a traitor? It should show.

HIPPOLYTE

Puis-je vous demander quel funeste nuage,
Seigneur, a pu troubler votre auguste visage?
N'osez-vous confier ce secret à ma foi?

THÉSÉE

Perfide! oses-tu bien te montrer devant moi?
Monstre, qu'a trop longtemps épargné le tonnerre,
Reste impur des brigands dont j'ai purgé la terre.
Après que le transport d'un amour plein d'horreur
Jusqu'au lit de ton père a porté sa fureur,
Tu m'oses présenter une tête ennemie,
Tu parais dans des lieux pleins de ton infâmie,
Et ne vas pas chercher, sous un ciel inconnu,
Des pays où mon nom ne soit point parvenu.
Fuis, traître. Ne viens point braver ici ma haine,
Et tenter un courroux que je retiens à peine.
C'est bien assez pour moi de l'opprobre éternel
D'avoir pu mettre au jour un fils si criminel,
Sans que ta mort encor, honteuse à ma mémoire,
De mes nobles travaux vienne souiller la gloire.
Fuis; et si tu ne veux qu'un châtiment soudain
T'ajoute aux scélérats qu'a punis cette main,
Prends garde que jamais l'astre qui nous éclaire
Ne te voie en ces lieux mettre un pied téméraire.
Fuis, dis-je; et sans retour précipitant tes pas,
De ton horrible aspect purge tous mes États.
Et toi, Neptune, et toi, si jadis mon courage
D'infâmes assassins nettoya ton rivage,
Souviens-toi que pour prix de mes efforts heureux,
Tu promis d'exaucer le premier de mes vœux.
Dans les longues rigueurs d'une prison cruelle
Je n'ai point imploré ta puissance immortelle.
Avare du secours que j'attends de tes soins,
Mes vœux t'ont réservé pour de plus grands besoins.
Je t'implore aujourd'hui. Venge un malheureux père.

HIPPOLYTUS

My father, may I ask what fatal cloud
Has overspread your noble brow? Can you
Not trust this secret to my confidence?

THESEUS

Traitor. How dare you show yourself to me?
Monster whom Heaven's bolts have spared too long
Filthy survivor of that brigand crew
Of which I purged the earth! After your lust
Had forced its way even into my bed,
You dare to show your hated face to me!
You have the effrontery to bring yourself
Into this very place where all is full
Of your foul infamy. No, you should seek
Some unknown land that never heard my name!
Fly, traitor! Do not stay to brave my wrath:
An anger I can barely hold in check.
Disgrace enough for ever have I earn'd
By being father of so vile a son,
Without your death staining indelibly
The glorious record of my noble deeds.
Fly; and unless you wish quick punishment
To add you to the criminals cut off
By me, see that this sun that lights us now
Find you no more with foot upon this soil.
Fly, I say fly! Without a backward look,
With steps precipitate be gone from here;
Rid all my realms of the vile sight of you.
And Thou, oh Neptune, Thou, great God recall,
If ever it was I who cleared Thy shores
Of murderers, recall Thy promise given,
Thy promise to reward me for success
By granting my first prayer. I have refrained;
Even when long in cruel prison bound,
I did not call on Thy immortal power,
Miserly hoarding to the last Thy help
Till at my utmost need. I ask it now.

J'abandonne ce traître à toute ta colère;
Étouffe dans son sang ses désirs effrontés:
Thésée à tes fureurs connaîtra tes bontés.

HIPPOLYTE

D'un amour criminel Phèdre accuse Hippolyte!
Un tel excès d'horreur rend mon âme interdite;
Tant de coups imprévus m'accablent à la fois,
Qu'ils m'ôtent la parole et m'étouffent la voix.

THÉSÉE

Traître, tu prétendais qu'en un lâche silence
Phèdre ensevelirait ta brutale insolence.
Il fallait, en fuyant, ne pas abandonner
Le fer qui dans ses mains aide à te condamner;
Ou plutôt il fallait, comblant ta perfidie,
Lui ravir tout d'un coup la parole et la vie.

HIPPOLYTE

D'un mensonge si noir justement irrité,
Je devrais faire ici parler la vérité,
Seigneur, mais je supprime un secret qui vous touche.
Approuvez le respect qui me ferme la bouche;
Et sans vouloir vous-même augmenter vos ennuis,
Examinez ma vie et songez qui je suis.
Quelques crimes toujours précèdent les grands crimes.
Quiconque a pu franchir les bornes légitimes
Peut violer enfin les droits les plus sacrés;
Ainsi que la vertu, le crime a ses degrés;
Et jamais on n'a vu la timide innocence
Passer subitement à l'extrême licence.
Un jour seul ne fait point d'un mortel vertueux
Un perfide assassin, un lâche incestueux.
Élevé dans le sein d'une chaste héroïne,
Je n'ai point de son sang démenti l'origine.

Avenge a father grievously betrayed.
I leave this traitor to Thy wrath. In blood,
In his own blood drown his obscene desires!
Thy utmost fury I invoke and will
Think it but kindness if that fury kill.

HIPPOLYTUS

Phaedra accuses me of shameful love?
Such overpowering horror stuns my soul.
Such unexpected blows, falling at once
Take all words from me, stifle, choke my voice.

THESEUS

Traitor you thought that Phaedra would hush up
In cowardly silence your brutish attack.
You should not have abandoned in your flight
The sword that in her hands helps to condemn you.
Better to crown your perfidy you should
Have robbed her of both speech and life at once.

HIPPOLYTUS

Justly indignant at a lie so black
I ought, my Lord, to make the truth speak now.
But for your honour's sake I must suppress it.
Approve the reverence that muzzles me;
Without yourself augmenting your distress
Look at my life! My Lord, think who I am.
Small crimes ever precede the greater crimes.
He who has broken once the moral law
May end by violating all the rights
We hold most sacred. But, like virtue, crime
Has its degrees, and timid innocence
Was never seen in one jump to embrace
The extremity of license. No one day
Can make a virtuous man a murderer
Most vile, a traitor, and—*incestuous*.
A chaste, heroic mother brought me up.
I have not proved unworthy of my birth.

Pitthée, estimé sage entre tous les humains,
Daigna m'instruire encore au sortir de ses mains.
Je ne veux point me peindre avec trop d'avantage;
Mais si quelque vertu m'est tombée en partage,
Seigneur, je crois surtout avoir fait éclater
La haine des forfaits qu'on ose m'imputer.
C'est par là qu'Hippolyte est connu dans la Grèce.
J'ai poussé la vertu jusques à la rudesse.
On sait de mes chagrins l'inflexible rigueur.
Le jour n'est pas plus pur que le fond de mon cœur.
Et l'on veut qu'Hippolyte, épris d'un feu profane . . .

THÉSÉE

Oui, c'est ce même orgueil, lâche! qui te condamne.
Je vois de tes froideurs le principe odieux:
Phèdre seule charmait tes impudiques yeux;
Et pour tout autre objet ton âme indifférente
Dédaignait de brûler d'une flamme innocente.

HIPPOLYTE

Non, mon père, ce cœur, c'est trop vous le celer,
N'a point d'un chaste amour dédaigné de brûler.
Je confesse à vos pieds ma véritable offense:
J'aime; j'aime, il est vrai, malgré votre défense.
Aricie à ses lois tient mes vœux asservis;
La fille de Pallante a vaincu votre fils.
Je l'adore, et mon âme, à vos ordres rebelle,
Ne peut ni soupirer ni brûler que pour elle.

THÉSÉE

Tu l'aimes? ciel! Mais non, l'artifice est grossier.
Tu te feins criminel pour te justifier.

Pittheus, considered wisest of all men,
Deigned to instruct me when I left her hands.
It is no wish of mine to paint myself
In a too favourable light, but if
A share at all of virtue fell to me,
I think beyond all else I have displayed
A hatred of those very sins it seems
Someone has dared impute to me. It is
For this Hippolytus is known in Greece:
For virtue so extreme as to be harsh.
And my inflexible, my rigorous
Austerity is known, is known to all.
The very light of day is not more pure
Than my heart's core. Can anyone believe
My name linked with illicit love . . .

THESEUS

                              Oh yes!
Coward, you are condemned by that same pride.
I see the odious reason now for your
Cold character. Phaedra alone could tempt
Your shameless eyes, and, to all other charms
Indifferent, your heart refused to burn
With fires of innocent love.

HIPPOLYTUS

                    No, Father, no!
It is too much to hide from you. This heart
Has not refused to burn with sacred flame.
Here, at your feet, I own my real offence,
I love, and love it's true, where you forbade:
Aricia has me captive, vanquished; she,
The daughter of Pallas! To your decree,
My soul, a rebel, only breathes and burns
For her, for her alone—her I adore.

THESEUS

You love her? Heav'ns! But no, the trick is crude.
You feign a crime to justify yourself.

HIPPOLYTE

Seigneur, depuis six mois je l'évite, et je l'aime.
Je venais en tremblant vous le dire à vous-même.
Hé quoi? de votre erreur rien ne vous peut tirer?
Par quel affreux serment faut-il vous rassurer?
Que la terre, le ciel, que toute la nature . . .

THÉSÉE

Toujours les scélérats ont recours au parjure.
Cesse, cesse, et m'épargne un importun discours,
Si ta fausse vertu n'a point d'autre secours.

HIPPOLYTE

Elle vous paraît fausse et pleine d'artifice.
Phèdre au fond de son cœur me rend plus de justice.

THÉSÉE

Ah! que ton impudence excite mon courroux!

HIPPOLYTE

Quel temps à mon exil, quel lieu prescrivez-vous?

THÉSÉE

Fusses-tu par delà les colonnes d'Alcide,
Je me croirais encor trop voisin d'un perfide.

HIPPOLYTE

Chargé du crime affreux dont vous me soupçonnez,
Quels amis me plaindront, quand vous m'abandonnez?

THÉSÉE

Va chercher des amis dont l'estime funeste
Honore l'adultère, applaudisse à l'inceste,
Des traîtres, des ingrats sans honneur et sans loi,
Dignes de protéger un méchant tel que toi.

HIPPOLYTUS

Sir, for six months I have avoided her
And still love her. To you I trembling came
To tell the news. Can nothing drag your mind
From its mistake? What oath is fierce enough
To reassure you? Let this earth, the heavens,
And all the powers of Nature . . .

THESEUS

                              Criminals
Have perjury upon a ready tongue.
Spare me these irksome protestations. Cease.
If your false virtue have no other aid.

HIPPOLYTUS

Though it seem false and insincere to you,
Phaedra will do me justice in her heart.

THESEUS

Ah! How your shamelessness excites my wrath!

HIPPOLYTUS

Where is my place of exile, and how long?

THESEUS

Were you beyond the pillars of Alcides
I should find such a traitor still too near.

HIPPOLYTUS

What friends will pity me when you forsake,
When you accuse me of so foul a crime?

THESEUS

Go, look for friends who hold in high esteem
Adultery, and who applaud incest.
Traitors who know no law nor gratitude
Nor honour—fit protectors for a wretch
Like you.

Vous me parlez toujours d'inceste et d'adultère?
Je me tais. Cependant Phèdre sort d'une mère,
Phèdre est d'un sang, Seigneur, vous le savez trop bien,
De toutes ces horreurs plus rempli que le mien.

THÉSÉE

Quoi? ta rage à mes yeux perd toute retenue?
Pour la dernière fois, ôte-toi de ma vue:
Sors, traître. N'attends pas qu'un père furieux
Te fasse avec opprobre arracher de ces lieux.

SCÈNE 3

Thésée, seul

Misérable, tu cours à ta perte infaillible.
Neptune, par le fleuve aux Dieux même terrible,
M'a donné sa parole et va l'exécuter.
Un Dieu vengeur te suit, tu ne peux l'éviter.
Je t'aimais; et je sens que malgré ton offense
Mes entrailles pour toi se troublent par avance.
Mais à te condamner tu m'as trop engagé.
Jamais père en effet fut-il plus outragé?
Justes Dieux, qui voyez la douleur qui m'accable,
Ai-je pu mettre au jour un enfant si coupable?

SCÈNE 4

Phèdre, Thésée

PHÈDRE

Seigneur, je viens à vous, pleine d'un juste effroi.

HIPPOLYTUS

Adultery and incest still
The words you use! I hold my tongue. Yet think,
Reflect what mother Phaedra had! What blood
Is hers! You know it, all too well, my Lord,
More tainted with these horrors than is mine.

THESEUS

What! Face to face with me, you let your rage
Lose all restraint? For the last time, begone
Out of my sight! Traitor, out of my sight!
And do not wait until a father's wrath
Have you dragged hence in execration.

SCENE 3

Theseus, alone

Oh miserable boy, you run to meet
Your end—inevitable. Neptune swore
By that dark river, to the Gods themselves
A source of terror; he has given me
A promise and it will be kept. Divine
Revenge pursues you. You have no escape.
I loved you, and in spite of your offence,
My heart anticipates your end and yearns
For you. But you have too well earned your doom.
Was ever father more offended? Gods,
Who see the grief now overwhelming me,
Can I have fathered so depraved a child?

SCENE 4

Phaedra, Theseus

PHAEDRA

My Lord, I hasten to you filled with dread.

Votre voix redoutable a passé jusqu'à moi.
Je crains qu'un prompt effet n'ait suivi la menace.
S'il en est temps encore, épargnez votre race;
Respectez votre sang, j'ose vous en prier.
Sauvez-moi de l'horreur de l'entendre crier;
Ne me préparez point la douleur éternelle
De l'avoir fait répandre à la main paternelle.

THÉSÉE

Non, Madame, en mon sang ma main n'a point trempé.
Mais l'ingrat toutefois ne m'est point échappé.
Une immortelle main de sa perte est chargée.
Neptune me la doit, et vous serez vengée.

PHÈDRE

Neptune vous la doit! Quoi? vos vœux irrités . . .

THÉSÉE

Quoi? craignez-vous déjà qu'ils ne soient écoutés?
Joignez-vous bien plutôt à mes vœux légitimes.
Dans toute leur noirceur retracez-moi ses crimes;
Échauffez mes transports trop lents, trop retenus.
Tous ses crimes encor ne vous sont pas connus:
Sa fureur contre vous se répand en injures:
Votre bouche, dit-il, est pleine d'impostures;
Il soutient qu'Aricie a son cœur, a sa foi,
Qu'il l'aime.

PHÈDRE

Quoi! Seigneur?

THÉSÉE

Il l'a dit devant moi.
Mais je sais rejeter un frivole artifice.
Espérons de Neptune une prompte justice.

Your loud and fearful voice came through to me.
I fear lest instant deeds have followed threats.
Oh, if there still is time, spare your own child.
Have mercy on your race and blood I pray.
Save me the horror of the sound of that
Blood crying from the ground. Do not prepare
For me the everlasting misery
Of having caused his father's hand to shed it.

THESEUS

No, my own blood is not upon my hand.
But still the villain will not have escaped.
Immortal hands are now responsible
For his destruction. Neptune owes me that
A debt of honour. You shall be avenged.

PHAEDRA

A debt? Owed you? Prayers made in anger may . . .

THESEUS

What's this? Are you afraid they may be heard?
No, rather join your angry prayers to mine.
In all their blackness paint for me his crimes,
And rouse my wrath already far too slow,
Far too restrained. You do not know of all
His crimes as yet. His fury against you
Explodes in slanders; for, your mouth he says
Is filled with all deceit. Indeed he says,—
Insists—Aricia has his heart and soul
That he loves her alone.

PHAEDRA

What did you say?

THESEUS

He said it to my face. But well I know
How to reject so shallow a pretence.
Let us, from Neptune hope for instant justice.

131

Je vais moi-même encore au pied de ses autels
Le presser d'accomplir ses serments immortels.

SCÈNE 5

Phèdre, seule

Il sort. Quelle nouvelle a frappé mon oreille?
Quel feu mal étouffé dans mon cœur se réveille?
Quel coup de foudre, ô ciel! et quel funeste avis!
Je volais toute entière au secours de son fils;
Et m'arrachant des bras d'Œnone épouvantée,
Je cédais au remords dont j'étais tourmentée.
Qui sait même où m'allait porter ce repentir?
Peut-être à m'accuser j'aurais pu consentir;
Peut-être, si la voix ne m'eût été coupée,
L'affreuse vérité me serait échappée.
Hippolyte est sensible, et ne sent rien pour moi!
Aricie a son cœur! Aricie a sa foi!
Ah, Dieux! Lorsqu'à mes vœux l'ingrat inexorable
S'armait d'un œil si fier, d'un front si redoutable,
Je pensais qu'à l'amour son cœur toujours fermé
Fût contre tout mon sexe également armé.
Une autre cependant a fléchi son audace;
Devant ses yeux cruels une autre a trouvé grâce.
Peut-être a-t-il un cœur facile à s'attendrir.
Je suis le seul objet qu'il ne saurait souffrir;
Et je me chargerais du soin de le défendre?

SCÈNE 6

Phèdre, Œnone

PHÈDRE

Chère Œnone, sais-tu ce que je viens d'apprendre?

I'll go, myself, and at his altar's foot
Urge yet again performance of his oath,
The immortal oath he swore to me.

SCENE 5

Phaedra, alone

He's gone.
What tidings struck my ears? What ill-quenched fire
Revives within my heart? What thunderbolt!
What fatal news! Oh Heav'ns, when I flew here
With one intent—to save his son—when I
Tore off the frightened grasp of poor Œnone
And yielded to my torments of remorse,
Who knows? Perhaps I might have damned myself
With a self-accusation! Perhaps,
But for my words being cut off, I might
Have let escape from me the hideous truth.
Hippolytus can feel, but not for me.
Aricia has his heart. Aricia
His promised love. Oh Gods! When, undisturbed
By all my protestations he displayed
A frowning forehead and a scornful eye,
I thought his heart, impregnable to love,
Was proof against all my poor sex alike!
And yet, another has prevailed to tame him;
Someone has found favour in his eyes!
Perhaps he has a heart easily touched!
I am the only one he cannot bear!
And shall I charge myself with his defence?

SCENE 6

Phaedra, Œnone

PHAEDRA

Dear Nurse, do you know what I have just learned?

ŒNONE

Non, mais je viens tremblante, à ne vous point mentir.
J'ai pâli du dessein qui vous a fait sortir:
J'ai craint une fureur à vous-même fatale.

PHÈDRE

Œnone, qui l'eût cru? j'avais une rivale.

ŒNONE

Comment?

PHÈDRE

Hippolyte aime, et je n'en puis douter.
Ce farouche ennemi qu'on ne pouvait dompter,
Qu'offensait le respect, qu'importunait la plainte,
Ce tigre, que jamais je n'abordai sans crainte,
Soumis, apprivoisé, reconnaît un vainqueur:
Aricie a trouvé le chemin de son cœur.

ŒNONE

Aricie?

PHÈDRE

Ah! douleur non encore éprouvée!
A quel nouveau tourment je me suis réservée!
Tout ce que j'ai souffert, mes craintes, mes transports,
La fureur de mes feux, l'horreur de mes remords,
Et d'un refus cruel l'insupportable injure,
N'était qu'un faible essai du tourment que j'endure.
Ils s'aiment! Par quel charme ont-ils trompé mes yeux?
Comment se sont-ils vus? Depuis quand? Dans quels
    lieux?
Tu le savais. Pourquoi me laissais-tu séduire?
De leur furtive ardeur ne pouvais-tu m'instruire?

No, but to tell the truth, I come in fear
And trembling, lest what caused you to rush out
Should be a madness fatal to yourself.

PHAEDRA

Who would have thought it, Nurse, I had a rival?

ŒNONE

How?

PHAEDRA

 Yes—Hippolytus! He is in love.
I cannot doubt it. Wild, untameable,
Ferocious he,—who scorned to be admired,
Resented praise, hated to be revered,
Found pleas importunate—this tiger, he
Whom I so feared to rouse—submits,
And, tamed and suppliant, fawns upon a hand
He owns as conqueror! Aricia
Has found the way into that heart.

ŒNONE

       Aricia?

PHAEDRA

Ah, anguish as yet untried! What more?
For what new tortures am I still reserved?
All I have undergone, of ecstasies,
Of longings, fears, the horrors of remorse;
The intolerable shame of being spurned,
Were feeble foretastes of my torment now.
They love each other. By what guile have they
Deceived me? How did they contrive to meet?
Since when? And in what places? You knew all!
Why did you let them fool me? Could you not
Have told me of their stolen furtive hours
Of amorous discourse? Who saw them speak?

Les a-t-on vus souvent se parler, se chercher?
Dans le fond des forêts allaient-ils se cacher?
Hélas! Ils se voyaient avec pleine licence.
Le ciel de leurs soupirs approuvait l'innocence;
Ils suivaient sans remords leur penchant amoureux;
Tous les jours se levaient clairs et sereins pour eux.
Et moi, triste rebut de la nature entière,
Je me cachais au jour, je fuyais la lumière:
La mort est le seul dieu que j'osais implorer.
J'attendais le moment où j'allais expirer;
Me nourrissant de fiel, de larmes abreuvée,
Encor dans mon malheur de trop près observée,
Je n'osais dans mes pleurs me noyer à loisir;
Je goûtais en tremblant ce funeste plaisir;
Et sous un front serein déguisant mes alarmes,
Il fallait bien souvent me priver de mes larmes.

ŒNONE

Quel fruit recevront-ils de leurs vaines amours?
Ils ne se verront plus.

PHÈDRE

             Ils s'aimeront toujours.
Au moment que je parle, ah! mortelle pensée!
Ils bravent la fureur d'une amante insensée.
Malgré ce même exil qui va les écarter,
Ils font mille serments de ne se point quitter.
Non, je ne puis souffrir un bonheur qui m'outrage;
Œnone, prends pitié de ma jalouse rage.
Il faut perdre Aricie. Il faut de mon époux

How often were they seen to meet? To seek
Each other's company? And did they hide
In the dark forest's depths? Alas they saw
Each other with full licence! Heav'n approved
Their innocent vows. They followed the sweet course
Of amorous desire, unhindered, free;
And every morning's sun shone clear for them.
While I, outcast and fugitive from all
That Nature shows most natural, I had
To shun the day and hide myself from light.
Death was the only God whose aid I dared
Implore. I waited for the grave's release.
Thirst quenched with tears, with gall for nourishment,
Still was my misery so closely watched
I dared not even drown myself in tears.
I dared not weep—not even weep in peace!
Even this mournful pleasure was not mine
In freedom, but in trembling, secret fear.
I had to hide behind a smiling mask
My terror, and deprive myself of all—
Even of the poor solace of my tears.

ŒNONE

What good will their love do them? It is vain.
They will not see each other any more.

PHAEDRA

Their love will last for ever. While I speak—
Ah, savage thought—they challenge the despair
Of an infuriated lover! Even though
Doomed instantly to part by forced exile
They're making promises with oaths and vows
That they will never separate! Oh no!
I cannot bear their happiness, Œnone.
It is an insult to me, drives me mad.
Pity my jealousy! Aricia
Must be destroyed. My husband's former wrath

Contre un sang odieux réveiller le courroux.
Qu'il ne se borne pas à des peines légères:
Le crime de la sœur passe celui des frères.
Dans mes jaloux transports je le veux implorer.
Que fais-je? Où ma raison se va-t-elle égarer?
Moi jalouse! et Thésée est celui que j'implore!
Mon époux est vivant, et moi je brûle encore!
Pour qui? Quel est le cœur où prétendent mes vœux?
Chaque mot sur mon front fait dresser mes cheveux.
Mes crimes désormais ont comblé la mesure.
Je respire à la fois l'inceste et l'imposture.
Mes homicides mains, promptes à me venger,
Dans le sang innocent brûlent de se plonger.
Misérable! et je vis? et je soutiens la vue
De ce sacré soleil dont je suis descendue?
J'ai pour aïeul le père et le maître des Dieux;
Le ciel, tout l'univers est plein de mes aïeux.
Où me cacher? Fuyons dans la nuit infernale.
Mais que dis-je? mon père y tient l'urne fatale;
Le sort, dit-on, l'a mise en ses sévères mains:
Minos juge aux enfers tous les pâles humains.
Ah! combien frémira son ombre épouvantée,
Lorsqu'il verra sa fille à ses yeux présentée,
Contrainte d'avouer tant de forfaits divers,
Et des crimes peut-être inconnus aux enfers!
Que diras-tu, mon père, à ce spectacle horrible?
Je crois voir de ta main tomber l'urne terrible;
Je crois te voir, cherchant un supplice nouveau,
Toi-même de ton sang devenir le bourreau.
Pardonne. Un Dieu cruel a perdu ta famille;
Reconnais sa vengeance aux fureurs de ta fille.
Hélas! du crime affreux dont la honte me suit
Jamais mon triste cœur n'a recueilli le fruit.
Jusqu'au dernier soupir de malheurs poursuivie
Je rends dans les tourments une pénible vie.

Against a hateful stock must be revived.
Nor must he stop at a light punishment.
Her guilt surpasses all her brothers' guilt.
I will implore him in my jealous rage . . .
What am I doing? My mind has lost its way,
For I am jealous, and the aid I ask
I ask of Theseus! Theseus lives, and I
Still burn with love—for whom? What heart is this
On which my heart is set? At every word
My hair stands up with horror. Guilt has passed
All bounds. Hypocrisy and incest breathe
At once through all. My murderous hands are prompt
To vengeance; eager to spill innocent blood.
Do I yet live, wretch that I am, and dare
To face this holy sun from which I spring?
My father was the master of the Gods;
My ancestors fill all the Universe.
Where can I hide? In the dark realms below?
But there my father holds the fatal urn;
His hand awards the irrevocable doom;
Minos is judge of all the ghosts in hell.
Ah! How his shade will shudder with surprise
When he shall see his daughter brought before him,
Forced to confess sins of such varied dye;
Crimes, it may be, unknown to hell itself!
What wilt thou say, my father, at a sight
So horrible? In my mind's eye I see
The fateful urn crash from thy hand. I see
Thee seeking some unheard-of punishment
Thyself become my executioner.
Pardon! A cruel God has damned thy race,
Destroyed thy family. Oh recognize,
In thy poor daughter's frenzy, her revenge.
Alas, my sad heart never plucked the fruit
Of pleasure from the frightful crime of which
I stand accused and dogged by shame. Alas,
To my last gasping breath by griefs pursued,
I here surrender my tormented life.

Hé! repoussez, Madame, une injuste terreur.
Regardez d'un autre œil une excusable erreur.
Vous aimez. On ne peut vaincre sa destinée.
Par un charme fatal vous fûtes entraînée.
Est-ce donc un prodige inouï parmi nous?
L'amour n'a-t-il encore triomphé que de vous?
La faiblesse aux humains n'est que trop naturelle.
Mortelle, subissez le sort d'une mortelle.
Vous vous plaigniez d'un joug imposé dès longtemps.
Les Dieux même, les Dieux, de l'Olympe habitants,
Qui d'un bruit si terrible épouvantent les crimes,
Ont brûlé quelquefois de feux illégitimes.

Qu'entends-je? Quels conseils ose-t-on me donner?
Ainsi donc jusqu'au bout tu veux m'empoisonner,
Malheureuse? Voilà comme tu m'as perdue.
Au jour que je fuyais c'est toi qui m'a rendue.
Tes prières m'ont fait oublier mon devoir.
J'évitais Hippolyte, et tu me l'as fait voir.
De quoi te chargeais-tu? Pourquoi ta bouche impie
A-t-elle, en l'accusant, osé noircir sa vie?
Il en mourra peut-être, et d'un père insensé
Le sacrilège vœu peut-être est exaucé.
Je ne t'écoute plus. Va-t'en, monstre exécrable.
Va, laisse-moi le soin de mon sort déplorable.
Puisse le juste ciel dignement te payer!
Et puisse ton supplice à jamais effrayer
Tous ceux qui, comme toi, par de lâches adresses,
Des princes malheureux nourrissent les faiblesses,
Les poussent au penchant où leur cœur est enclin,
Et leur osent du crime aplanir le chemin,
Détestables flatteurs, présent le plus funeste
Que puisse faire aux rois la colère céleste!

Oh Madam, do reject such needless fear.
Look with an easier eye on your mistake.
You love. We cannot conquer destiny.
You were drawn on by fatal charm. Is that
Something unheard of? Do you think that Love
Has triumphed over you, and you alone?
Frailty is only natural to us
Poor human beings. You are mortal, so
To a poor mortal's lot submit. You fight
Against a fate imposed since time began.
The Gods themselves, even the Olympian Gods
Who with so great a noise reprove our crimes,
Have sometimes burned with these forbidden fires.

PHAEDRA

What do I hear? You dare advise me still?
Determined, to the last, to poison me?
You have destroyed me. I tried to escape,
You dragged me back to life; it was your prayers
Made me forget my duty; when I shunned
Hippolytus you made me see him. Why
Did you take charge? Why did your wicked mouth
Dare to accuse and blacken his sweet life?
It may be you have killed him. It may be
An angry father's sacrilegious prayer
Is granted even now! I will not hear
Another word. Go, execrable fiend.
Let me command my own poor fate at last.
May Heaven with justice pay you out! And may
Your punishment for ever terrify
All those like you who with base craft and guile
Feed the infirmities of Princes; push
Them down that slope to which their heart inclines,
And smooth for their poor feet the path of crime.
Oh filthy flatterers! Most fatal gift
That angry Heaven can bestow on Kings!

(Exit)

Ah! Dieux! pour la servir j'ai tout fait, tout quitté;
Et j'en reçois ce prix? Je l'ai bien mérité.

Oh Gods! To serve her I've done all, lost all;
And this is my reward. Deserved, deserved.

(*Exit*)

ACTE V

SCÈNE I

Hippolyte, Aricie

ARICIE

Quoi? vous pouvez vous taire en ce péril extrême?
Vous laissez dans l'erreur un père qui vous aime?
Cruel, si de mes pleurs méprisant le pouvoir,
Vous consentez sans peine à ne me plus revoir,
Partez, séparez-vous de la triste Aricie.
Mais du moins en partant assurez votre vie.
Défendez votre honneur d'un reproche honteux,
Et forcez votre père à révoquer ses vœux.
Il en est temps encor. Pourquoi, par quel caprice,
Laissez-vous le champ libre à votre accusatrice?
Éclaircissez Thésée.

HIPPOLYTE

           Hé! que n'ai-je point dit?
Ai-je dû mettre au jour l'opprobre de son lit?
Devais-je, en lui faisant un récit trop sincère,
D'une indigne rougeur couvrir le front d'un père?
Vous seule avez percé ce mystère odieux.
Mon cœur pour s'épancher n'a que vous et les Dieux.
Je n'ai pu vous cacher, jugez si je vous aime,
Tout ce que je voulais me cacher à moi-même.
Mais songez sous quel sceau je vous l'ai révélé.
Oubliez, s'il se peut, que je vous ai parlé,
Madame; et que jamais une bouche si pure
Ne s'ouvre pour conter cette horrible aventure.
Sur l'équité des Dieux osons nous confier:

ACT V

SCENE I

Hippolytus, Aricia

ARICIA

In peril so extreme are you content
To hold your tongue, and leave in ignorance
A loving father? Cruel—if you are—
Enough to scorn my powerless tears and leave
Aricia without a wrench, and say
Farewell for ever—say it then: Farewell!
But look at least to safety of your life!
Defend your honour from a shameful stain,
And force your father to revoke his prayer.
There is yet time. Why, and for what caprice
Leave the field clear to Phaedra's calumnies?
Let Theseus know the truth!

HIPPOLYTUS

                Alas, what more
Could I have said without revealing all
The shame of his dishonoured bed? Should I
In telling him a story all too frank
Make blush with shame my father and my king?
The odious truth is known to you alone.
My heart has been outpoured to none but you,
And to the Gods. I could not hide from you,
Judge how I love you—all that I would hide
Even from myself! But think under what seal
I have revealed the truth. Forget my words
If that be possible, and never let
So pure a mouth disclose so foul a tale.
The Gods are just: we put our trust in them.

Ils ont trop d'intérêt à me justifier;
Et Phèdre, tôt ou tard de son crime punie,
N'en saurait éviter la juste ignominie.
C'est l'unique respect que j'exige de vous.
Je permets tout le reste à mon libre courroux.
Sortez de l'esclavage où vous êtes réduite;
Osez me suivre, osez accompagner ma fuite;
Arrachez-vous d'un lieu funeste et profané,
Où la vertu respire un air empoisonné.
Profitez, pour cacher votre prompte retraite,
De la confusion que ma disgrâce y jette.
Je vous puis de la fuite assurer les moyens.
Vous n'avez jusqu'ici de gardes que les miens.
De puissants défenseurs prendront notre querelle;
Argos nous tend les bras, et Sparte nous appelle:
A nos amis communs portons nos justes cris;
Ne souffrons pas que Phèdre, assemblant nos débris,
Du trône paternel nous chasse l'un et l'autre,
Et promette à son fils ma dépouille et la vôtre.
L'occasion est belle, il la faut embrasser.
Quelle peur vous retient? Vous semblez balancer?
Votre seul intérêt m'inspire cette audace.
Quand je suis tout de feu, d'où vous vient cette glace?
Sur les pas d'un banni craignez-vous de marcher?

ARICIE

Hélas! qu'un tel exil, Seigneur, me serait cher!
Dans quels ravissements, à votre sort liée,
Du reste des mortels je vivrais oubliée!
Mais n'étant point unis par un lien si doux,
Me puis-je avec honneur dérober avec vous?

For their own honour they will vindicate
And justify me. As for Phaedra, she,
Sooner or later punished for her crime,
Will not escape her just ignominy.
The one obedience I must demand
Of you is silence. For the rest, I'll give
Free rein to righteous indignation.
Dare to escape from your captivity.
Dare to come with me; join my flight. Shake off
The shackles of this doomed and filthy place
Where virtue breathes a poisoned air, and take
Advantage, so to cover your retreat,
Of the confusion caused by my disgrace.
I can assure you of the means of flight.
As yet you have no other guards than mine;
But strong defenders will be on our side:
Argos spreads open arms, and Sparta calls us.
Let us cry out for help to all our friends.
Let us prevent the seizure of our rights:
Our shattered fortunes must not be allowed
To feed the greed of Phaedra who will chase
Us both from rightful thrones, and give her son
The promise of our titles, wealth and all.
We have the chance now: we must take it now!
What do you fear? You seem to hesitate.
For your sake only dare I be so rash.
When I am all on fire, why are you ice?
Are you afraid, afraid to follow me
Because I am a banished man?

ARICIA

How dear
To me would be such exile, Prince! What bliss,
My fate to yours united, so to live
By all the rest of mortals quite forgot.
But, not joined to you by a bond so sweet,
How can I steal away without disgrace?
Enforced obedience may be shed, I know,

Je sais que, sans blesser l'honneur le plus sévère,
Je me puis affranchir des mains de votre père:
Ce n'est point m'arracher du sein de mes parents;
Et la fuite est permise à qui fuit ses tyrans.
Mais vous m'aimez, Seigneur; et ma gloire alarmée . . .

HIPPOLYTE

Non, non, j'ai trop de soin de votre renommée.
Un plus noble dessein m'amène devant vous:
Fuyez vos ennemis, et suivez votre époux.
Libres dans nos malheurs, puisque le ciel l'ordonne,
Le don de notre foi ne dépend de personne.
L'hymen n'est point toujours entouré de flambeaux.
Aux portes de Trézène, et parmi ces tombeaux,
Des princes de ma race antiques sépultures,
Est un temple sacré, formidable aux parjures.
C'est là que les mortels n'osent jurer en vain.
Le perfide y reçoit un châtiment soudain;
Et craignant d'y trouver la mort inévitable,
Le mensonge n'a point de frein plus redoutable.
Là, si vous m'en croyez, d'un amour éternel
Nous irons confirmer le serment solennel;
Nous prendrons à témoin le Dieu qu'on y révère;
Nous le prîrons tous deux de nous servir de père.
Des Dieux les plus sacrés j'attesterai le nom.
Et la chaste Diane, et l'auguste Junon,
Et tous les Dieux enfin, témoins de mes tendresses,
Garantiront la foi de mes saintes promesses.

ARICIE

Le Roi vient. Fuyez, Prince, et partez promptement.
Pour cacher mon départ je demeure un moment.

Without dishonour to the strictest law;
And from your father's hands I may escape.
This is not, never was, my parents' home.
To fly could not be called elopement! All
Are free to fly from tyranny. But you,
Have said you love me, and my virtue shrinks . . .

HIPPOLYTUS

No, no, I care too much for your good name.
A nobler plan I bring: fly from your foes
And follow me—your husband. Free at least
In our distress, since Heaven wills it so,
Our marriage vows depend on none but us,
Ourselves. True marriage is not always lit
By ceremonial torches. Just outside
The gates of Trozene, amid sepulchres
Where Princes of my race, my ancestors
Lie buried in their ancient tombs: there stands
A sacred temple dangerous to th' approach
Of perjurers; where mortals dare not take
An oath in falsity, for those forsworn
Receive an instant punishment of death,
Inevitable death. To liars all
This is the final judgement. There we'll go,
If you believe me, swear to love for ever;
Pledge our solemn vows before that God
Who there is worshipped. He will be to us
A witness, and a father to us both.
I will invoke the sacred name of all
The greatest of the Gods: Diana chaste;
Majestic Juno; all those Gods who are
And have been witness of my tender love.
And they will guarantee my faith, my truth,
My holy promises to you—my love.

ARICIA

The King draws near. Depart. Make no delay.
To mask my flight I'll stay one moment more.

149

Allez; et laissez-moi quelque fidèle guide,
Qui conduise vers vous ma démarche timide.

SCÈNE 2

Thésée, Aricie, Ismène

THÉSÉE

Dieux! éclairez mon trouble, et daignez à mes yeux
Montrer la vérité que je cherche en ces lieux.

ARICIE

Songe à tout, chère Ismène, et sois prête à la fuite.

SCÈNE 3

Thésée, Aricie

THÉSÉE

Vous changez de couleur et semblez interdite,
Madame. Que faisait Hippolyte en ce lieu?

ARICIE

Seigneur, il me disait un éternel adieu.

THÉSÉE

Vos yeux ont su dompter ce rebelle courage,
Et ses premiers soupirs sont votre heureux ouvrage.

ARICIE

Seigneur, je ne vous puis nier la vérité:
De votre injuste haine il n'a pas hérité;
Il ne me traitait point comme une criminelle.

You go: and leave with me some trusty guide
To lead my timid footsteps to your side.

SCENE 2

Theseus, Aricia, Ismene

THESEUS

Oh Gods! Throw light upon my troubled mind.
Show me the truth I search for in this place.

ARICIA

Get ready, dear Ismene, all we need,
And be at hand prepared for instant flight.

SCENE 3

Theseus, Aricia

THESEUS

Your colour changes, Madam, and you seem
Tongue-tied. Why was Hippolytus with you?

ARICIA

Sire, he was taking a last leave of me.

THESEUS

Your eyes, it seems have tamed that stubborn heart,
And the first sighs of love he ever breathed
It seems are your glad handiwork!

ARICIA

              My Lord,
To you I'll not deny it is the truth;
For he has not inherited your hate.
He has not treated me as criminal.

THÉSÉE

J'entends: il vous jurait une amour éternelle.
Ne vous assurez point sur ce cœur inconstant;
Car à d'autres que vous il en jurait autant.

ARICIE

Lui, Seigneur?

THÉSÉE

            Vous deviez le rendre moins volage.
Comment souffriez-vous cet horrible partage?

ARICIE

Et comment souffrez-vous que d'horribles discours
D'une si belle vie osent noircir le cours?
Avez-vous de son cœur si peu de connaissance?
Discernez-vous si mal le crime et l'innocence?
Faut-il qu'à vos yeux seuls un nuage odieux
Dérobe sa vertu qui brille à tous les yeux?
Ah! c'est trop le livrer à des langues perfides.
Cessez: repentez-vous de vos vœux homicides;
Craignez, Seigneur, craignez que le ciel rigoureux
Ne vous haïsse assez pour exaucer vos vœux.
Souvent dans sa colère il reçoit nos victimes;
Ses présents sont souvent la peine de nos crimes.

THÉSÉE

Non, vous voulez en vain couvrir son attentat:
Votre amour vous aveugle en faveur de l'ingrat.
Mais j'en crois des témoins certains, irréprochables:
J'ai vu, j'ai vu couler des larmes véritables.

ARICIE

Prenez garde, Seigneur. Vos invincibles mains
Ont de monstres sans nombre affranchi les humains;

152

THESEUS

I understand. He swore eternal love!
Do not rely on that inconstant heart.
He swore as much to others.

ARICIA

He, my Lord?

THESEUS

You should have curbed that fickle nature. How
Could you endure to share him? Horrible.

ARICIA

And how can you endure that horrible,
Vile words dare blacken such a lovely life?
Have you so little knowledge of his heart?
Can you so ill distinguish between guilt
And innocence? Why must some hideous cloud
Before your eyes, alone of all men's, hide
A virtue shining bright as day? Ah, no,
It is too much to leave him to false tongues.
Stop, stop! Repent! Call back your murderous prayer!
Fear, my Lord, fear lest Heaven, in revenge,
Hate you enough to grant your prayer! For Heaven
Often accepts our victims in its wrath,
And often when it grants our prayers its gifts
Are punishments of crime.

THESEUS

No! You, in vain
Are trying to conceal his foul attack.
Your love blinds you to his ingratitude
But I have witnesses that I can trust:
I have seen tears, I have seen true tears shed.

ARICIA

Take care, my Lord. Your conquering hands have freed
All mortals from the fear of countless foes:

153

Mais tout n'est pas détruit, et vous en laissez vivre
Un. . . . Votre fils, Seigneur, me défend de poursuivre.
Instruite du respect qu'il veut vous conserver,
Je l'affligerais trop si j'osais achever.
J'imite sa pudeur, et fuis votre présence
Pour n'être pas forcée à rompre le silence.

SCÈNE 4

Thésée, seul

Quelle est donc sa pensée? et que cache un discours
Commencé tant de fois, interrompu toujours?
Veulent-ils m'éblouir par une feinte vaine?
Sont-ils d'accord tous deux pour me mettre à la gêne?
Mais moi-même, malgré ma sévère rigueur,
Quelle plaintive voix crie au fond de mon cœur?
Une pitié secrète et m'afflige et m'étonne.
Une seconde fois interrogeons Œnone.
Je veux de tout le crime être mieux éclairci.
Gardes, qu'Œnone sorte, et vienne seule ici.

SCÈNE 5

Thésée, Panope

PANOPE

J'ignore le projet que la Reine médite,
Seigneur, mais je crains tout du transport qui l'agite.
Un mortel désespoir sur son visage est peint;
La pâleur de la mort est déjà sur son teint.
Déjà, de sa présence avec honte chassée,
Dans la profonde mer Œnone s'est lancée.
On ne sait point d'où part ce dessein furieux;
Et les flots pour jamais l'ont ravie à nos yeux.

Innumerable monsters. But not all
Have you destroyed. You have allowed to live
One . . . But your son, my Lord, forbids my speech.
Knowing the reverence he owes to you,
I should, if I went on, grieve him too much.
So I will imitate his reticence
And, to keep silence, fly your presence, Sire.

SCENE 4

Theseus, alone

What does she think, suspect? What hides beneath
A speech begun and often broken short?
Do they both wish to dazzle me with lies?
Are they in league to torture me? And yet
Though my severity is right and just
What voice, what plaintive voice cries from my heart?
I find I am afflicted and surprised
By a compassion that invades my soul.
Œnone must be questioned once again.
I must have clearer light upon this crime.
Guards! Fetch Œnone. Let her come alone.

SCENE 5

Theseus, Panope

PANOPE

I do not know what the Queen means to do
But from her violent mood fear anything.
Mortal despair is painted on her face
Death's pallor is already on her, Sir!
Œnone, driven from her sight in shame,
Has thrown herself into the deep sea. Why?
No one knows why she did a thing so mad,
But now the waves hide her from us for ever.

Qu'entends-je?

PANOPE

Son trépas n'a point calmé la Reine;
Le trouble semble croître en son âme incertaine.
Quelquefois, pour flatter ses secrètes douleurs,
Elle prend ses enfants et les baigne de pleurs;
Et soudain, renonçant à l'amour maternelle,
Sa main avec horreur les repousse loin d'elle.
Elle porte au hasard ses pas irrésolus;
Son œil tout égaré ne nous reconnaît plus.
Elle a trois fois écrit; et changeant de pensée,
Trois fois elle a rompu sa lettre commencée.
Daignez la voir, Seigneur; daignez la secourir.

THÉSÉE

O ciel! Œnone est morte, et Phèdre veut mourir?
Qu'on rappelle mon fils, qu'il vienne se défendre!
Qu'il vienne me parler, je suis prêt de l'entendre.
Ne précipite point tes funestes bienfaits,
Neptune; j'aime mieux n'être exaucé jamais.
J'ai peut-être trop cru des témoins peu fidèles,
Et j'ai trop tôt vers toi levé mes mains cruelles.
Ah! de quel désespoir mes vœux seraient suivis!

SCÈNE 6

Thésée, Théramène

THÉSÉE

Théramène, est-ce toi? Qu'as-tu fait de mon fils?
Je te l'ai confié dès l'âge le plus tendre.

What are you saying?

PANOPE

                    Sire, Œnone's death
Has brought no solace to the Queen, whose griefs
Seem to increase in her uncertain mind.
Sometimes to soothe her secret pain she clasps
Her children; bathes them with her tears, and then
Forgetting all her mother-love, her hand
Repulses them with horror far from her.
She wanders to and fro with doubtful steps;
Her vacant eyes no longer know us, Sire.
Three times she wrote a letter, and three times
She changed her mind, and tore it up, when, Sire,
It was not well begun! Consent to help,
Consent to see her, Sire.

THESEUS

                    Oh Heaven!
Œnone dead, and Phaedra bent on death!
Oh let them call him back! My son! Return!
Oh speak to me and this time I will hear.
Oh stay Thy hand, do not precipitate
Thy fatal gifts upon me, Neptune! Let
All prayers of mine for ever be unheard.
Did I believe false witnesses? Too soon
Did I raise cruel hands? Oh what despair
May follow.

SCENE 6

Theseus, Theramenes

THESEUS

            Is that you, Theramenes?
Where is my son? What have you done with him?
I trusted you—I trusted you with him

Mais d'où naissent les pleurs que je te vois répandre?
Que fait mon fils?

THÉRAMÈNE

O soins tardifs et superflus!
Inutile tendresse! Hippolyte n'est plus.

THÉSÉE

Dieux!

THÉRAMÈNE

J'ai vu des mortels périr le plus aimable,
Et j'ose dire encor, Seigneur, le moins coupable.

THÉSÉE

Mon fils n'est plus? Hé quoi? quand je lui tends les bras,
Les Dieux impatients ont hâté son trépas?
Quel coup me l'a ravi? quelle foudre soudaine?

THÉRAMÈNE

A peine nous sortions des portes de Trézène,
Il était sur son char; ses gardes affligés
Imitaient son silence, autour de lui rangés;
Il suivait tout pensif le chemin de Mycènes;
Sa main sur ses chevaux laissait flotter les rênes.
Ses superbes coursiers, qu'on voyait autrefois
Pleins d'une ardeur si noble obéir à sa voix,
L'œil morne maintenant et la tête baissée,
Semblaient se conformer à sa triste pensée.
Un effroyable cri, sorti du fond des flots,
Des airs en ce moment a troublé le repos;
Et du sein de la terre une voix formidable
Répond en gémissant à ce cri redoutable.

158

From tenderest childhood. What are these
Tears flowing from your eyes? Theramenes,
How is it with my son?

THERAMENES

                Too late, too late!
Oh tardy and superfluous concern!
Oh futile tenderness! Hippolytus
Is dead.

THESEUS

    Gods!

THERAMENES

               I have seen the flower—
Most lovable, least guilty of all men—
Cut down, and I am bold to tell you, Sire,
That none did ever less deserve his fate.

THESEUS

My son is dead? When I am holding out
My arms to him. Did the impatient Gods
Hasten his end? What was this thunderbolt?

THERAMENES

Just through the gates of Trozene we had passed,
He standing in his chariot; his sad guards,
Imitating his silence, round him ranged;
So, deep in thought, down the Mycenian road
He went; his hand allowed the reins to float
Loose on the horses' backs; his chargers once
So proud and eager to obey his voice,
With downcast head and melancholy eye,
Now seemed to suit their gait to his sad thoughts.
A frightful cry that issues from the deep
With sudden discord rends the troubled air,
And from the bosom of the earth a voice
Echoes in hideous groans that monstrous cry.

Jusqu'au fond de nos cœurs notre sang s'est glacé;
Des coursiers attentifs le crin s'est hérissé.
Cependant sur le dos de la plaine liquide
S'élève à gros bouillons une montagne humide;
L'onde approche, se brise, et vomit à nos yeux,
Parmi des flots d'écume, un monstre furieux.
Son front large est armé de cornes menaçantes;
Tout son corps est couvert d'écailles jaunissantes;
Indomptable taureau, dragon impétueux,
Sa croupe se recourbe en replis tortueux.
Ses longs mugissements font trembler le rivage.
Le ciel avec horreur voit ce monstre sauvage;
La terre s'en émeut, l'air en est infecté;
Le flot, qui l'apporta, recule épouvanté.
Tout fuit; et sans s'armer d'un courage inutile,
Dans le temple voisin chacun cherche un asile.
Hippolyte lui seul, digne fils d'un héros,
Arrête ses coursiers, saisit ses javelots,
Pousse au monstre, et d'un dard lancé d'une main sûre,
Il lui fait dans le flanc une large blessure.
De rage et de douleur le monstre bondissant
Vient aux pieds des chevaux tomber en mugissant,
Se roule, et leur présente une gueule enflammée,
Qui les couvre de feu, de sang et de fumée.
La frayeur les emporte; et sourds à cette fois,
Ils ne connaissent plus ni le frein ni la voix.
En efforts impuissants leur maître se consume;
Ils rougissent le mors d'une sanglante écume.
On dit qu'on a vu même, en ce désordre affreux,
Un Dieu qui d'aiguillons pressait leur flanc poudreux.
A travers les rochers la peur les précipite;
L'essieu crie et se rompt. L'intrépide Hippolyte
Voit voler en éclats tout son char fracassé;
Dans les rênes lui-même il tombe embarrassé.

Blood freezes at the bottom of our hearts.
With bristling manes the listening horses stand.
Meanwhile, upon the watery plain upheaves
A mountain billow with a mighty crest
Of foam that shoreward rolls, and as it breaks
Before our eyes spews forth a furious beast,
A monster armed with terrifying horns,
And all its body clothed with yellow scales:
A thing at once indomitable bull
And darting dragon whose hind-quarters lashed
And twisted down in hideous slimy coils.
Its long-drawn bellowings shake the shore; the sky
Seems watching horror-struck at such a sight;
The earth quakes and the air is poisoned. Then
The wave that brought it ebbs away in fear.
All run away, abandoning in flight
The very thought of useless bravery;
Take refuge in the temple close at hand.
All but Hippolytus—a hero's son
And worthy to be so—he stays his steeds,
Seizes his javelins, charges at the beast,
And with a dart sped from a steady hand
Makes in its flank a deep and grievous wound.
With rage and pain the monster somersaults
Right to the horses' feet and bellowing falls,
Writhes in the dust and shows a fiery throat
That covers them with flames and blood and smoke.
Then terror carries them away, and deaf,
They do not hear his voice nor feel his hands.
Their master wastes his unavailing strength;
They make a bloody foam upon their bit.
Some even claim that in this disarray
A God was seen spurring their dusty sides.
Over the rocks fear hurtles them, and—crash!
The axle-tree screams, snaps and breaks! And he
The intrepid youth Hippolytus now sees
His chariot splinter into bits. He falls
Himself at last, entangled in the reins.

Excusez ma douleur. Cette image cruelle
Sera pour moi de pleurs une source éternelle.
J'ai vu, Seigneur, j'ai vu votre malheureux fils
Traîné par les chevaux que sa main a nourris.
Il veut les rappeler et sa voix les effraie;
Ils courent. Tout son corps n'est bientôt qu'une plaie.
De nos cris douloureux la plaine retentit.
Leur fougue impétueuse enfin se ralentit:
Ils s'arrêtent, non loin de ces tombeaux antiques
Où des rois ses aïeux sont les froides reliques.
J'y cours en soupirant, et sa garde me suit.
De son généreux sang la trace nous conduit:
Les rochers en sont teints; les ronces dégouttantes
Portent de ses cheveux les dépouilles sanglantes.
J'arrive, je l'appelle; et me tendant la main,
Il ouvre un œil mourant, qu'il referme soudain.
'Le ciel, dit-il, m'arrache une innocente vie.
Prends soin après ma mort de la triste Aricie.
Cher ami, si mon père un jour désabusé
Plaint le malheur d'un fils faussement accusé,
Pour apaiser mon sang et mon ombre plaintive,
Dis-lui qu'avec douceur il traite sa captive;
Qu'il lui rende . . .' A ce mot ce héros expiré
N'a laissé dans mes bras qu'un corps défiguré,
Triste objet, où des Dieux triomphe la colère,
Et que méconnaîtrait l'œil même de son père.

THÉSÉE

O mon fils! cher espoir que je me suis ravi!
Inexorables Dieux, qui m'avez trop servi!
A quels mortels regrets ma vie est réservée!

THÉRAMÈNE

La timide Aricie est alors arrivée.
Elle venait, Seigneur, fuyant votre courroux.

Forgive my grief. That cruel sight will be
For me an everlasting source of tears.
I saw, I saw him, your unhappy son
Dragged by the horses that his hands had fed.
He tries to call them back. Alas, his voice
Adds to their fright. They gallop headlong on.
His body is one single wound. The plains
Re-echo with our miserable cries.
At last their mad pace slackens, and they stop
Not far from those old tombs which make of those,
His ancestors, the last cold resting-place.
Sobbing I run there; following me,
His guards. Along the track his generous blood
Leads us. The rocks are red. Caught in the briars
Remains of locks of hair hang dripping blood.
I come; I call him. Stretching forth his hand,
He opens dying eyes, soon closed again.
'The Gods have robbed me of a guiltless life,'
I hear him say. 'Take care, after my death,
Take care of sad Aricia; and if
One day my father learns the truth, and if
He mourns his slandered son's unhappy fate:
To give my blood and plaintive ghost repose,
Ask him to treat his captive tenderly;
And to restore . . .' At this he died,
And in my arms left his disfigured corpse;
A piteous object, victim of the wrath
Of Gods, so changed his father would not know him.

THESEUS

My son. My son. Dear hope I have destroyed!
Inexorable Gods who have too well
Served me, to what an everlasting grief
I am ordained.

THERAMENES
And then upon the scene
Comes shy Aricia, in flight from you,

A la face des Dieux l'accepter pour époux.
Elle approche: elle voit l'herbe rouge et fumante;
Elle voit (quel objet pour les yeux d'une amante!)
Hippolyte étendu, sans forme et sans couleur.
Elle veut quelque temps douter de son malheur;
Et ne connaissant plus ce héros qu'elle adore,
Elle voit Hippolyte, et le demande encore.
Mais trop sûre à la fin qu'il est devant ses yeux,
Par un triste regard elle accuse les Dieux;
Et froide, gémissante, et presque inanimée,
Aux pieds de son amant elle tombe pâmée.
Ismène est auprès d'elle; Ismène, toute en pleurs,
La rappelle à la vie, ou plutôt aux douleurs.
Et moi, je suis venu, détestant la lumière,
Vous dire d'un héros la volonté dernière,
Et m'acquitter, Seigneur, du malheureux emploi
Dont son cœur expirant s'est reposé sur moi.
Mais j'aperçois venir sa mortelle ennemie.

SCÈNE 7

Thésée, Phèdre, Théramène, Panope, Gardes

THÉSÉE

Hé bien! vous triomphez, et mon fils est sans vie.
Ah! que j'ai lieu de craindre! et qu'un cruel soupçon,
L'excusant dans mon cœur, m'alarme avec raison!
Mais, Madame, il est mort, prenez votre victime:
Jouissez de sa perte, injuste ou légitime.
Je consens que mes yeux soient toujours abusés.
Je le crois criminel, puisque vous l'accusez.
Son trépas à mes pleurs offre assez de matières,
Sans que j'aille chercher d'odieuses lumières,
Qui ne pouvant le rendre à ma juste douleur,
Peut-être ne feraient qu'accroître mon malheur.

Meaning to marry him before the Gods.
So she approaches, sees the grass all red
And steaming with hot blood—think what a sight
For lover's eyes—Hippolytus stretched out
Shapeless and colourless, disfigured, dead.
She, for a time, will not believe her loss.
No longer recognizing him, her love,
She sees Hippolytus and asks for him!
But all too sure at last that he lies there
Before her eyes, she casts a mournful look
Of accusation at the Gods, and falls
Cold, shivering, groaning, at her lover's feet.
Ismene is beside her, drowned in tears,
And calls her back to life, or rather back
To grief. And I, detesting now the light,
Come to make you a hero's last request,
And so perform the miserable task
His dying heart imposed on me, his friend.
But here is now his mortal enemy.

SCENE 7

Theseus, Theramenes, Phaedra, Panope, Guards

THESEUS

You have your triumph and my son is killed.
And yet, what room I have for fear! How right
The insidious suspicion in my heart
Which made excuses for him, warning me.
But, Madam, he is dead. Accept your prey
Rightly or wrongly killed; you may rejoice.
My eyes, I'll grant, shall be for ever blind.
Since you accuse him, I'll believe his guilt.
His death affords me cause enough for tears
Without a foolish search for further light,
Which, powerless to give him back to me,
Might only add more grief to my despair.

Laissez-moi, loin de vous et loin de ce rivage,
De mon fils déchiré fuir la sanglante image.
Confus, persécuté d'un mortel souvenir,
De l'univers entier je voudrais me bannir.
Tout semble s'élever contre mon injustice.
L'éclat de mon nom même augmente mon supplice.
Moins connu des mortels, je me cacherai mieux.
Je hais jusques au soin dont m'honorent les Dieux;
Et je m'en vais pleurer leurs faveurs meurtrières,
Sans plus les fatiguer d'inutiles prières.
Quoi qu'ils fissent pour moi, leur funeste bonté
Ne me saurait payer de ce qu'ils m'ont ôté.

PHÈDRE

Non, Thésée, il faut rompre un injuste silence:
Il faut à votre fils rendre son innocence.
Il n'était point coupable.

THÉSÉE

        Ah! père infortuné!
Et c'est sur votre foi que je l'ai condamné!
Cruelle, pensez-vous être assez excusée . . .

PHÈDRE

Les moments me sont chers, écoutez-moi, Thésée.
C'est moi qui sur ce fils chaste et respectueux
Osai jeter un œil profane, incestueux.
Le ciel mit dans mon sein une flamme funeste;
La détestable Œnone a conduit tout le reste.
Elle a craint qu'Hippolyte, instruit de ma fureur,
Ne découvrit un feu qui lui faisait horreur.
La perfide, abusant de ma faiblesse extrême,

Let me, far from this shore, and far from you
Escape the image of my mangled son.
Hounded for ever by this memory,
From the whole universe I long to hide
And banish me. The whole world seems to rise
In anger at injustice. And my fame
Itself adds to my condemnation,
For were my name less famous I would be
An easier thing to hide. I hate the care
With which the Gods have honoured me. I'll go.
Their murderous favours I'll for ever mourn.
I will not tire them with my prayers again.
Whatever they have done for me, I say,
What they have taken will all else outweigh.

PHAEDRA

No, Theseus: I must break this unjust silence:
Must restore your son's lost innocence:
He was not guilty.

THESEUS

    Oh unhappy father!
And it was on your word that I condemned
Him. Cruelty beyond excuse . . .

PHAEDRA

      Theseus
Moments to me are precious. Listen now.
Phaedra it was who dared to look with love
Profane—incestuous—upon that chaste
And dutiful Hippolytus, your son.
Heaven in my heart kindled the fatal flame
Detestable Œnone did the rest.
She must have feared that he, Hippolytus,
Knowing my madness, might reveal my love
Which he refused with horror. So she took
Perfidious advantage of my state
Of deathly weakness and made haste to you

S'est hâtée à vos yeux de l'accuser lui-même.
Elle s'en est punie, et, fuyant mon courroux,
A cherché dans les flots un supplice trop doux.
Le fer aurait déjà tranché ma destinée;
Mais je laissais gémir la vertu soupçonnée.
J'ai voulu, devant vous exposant mes remords,
Par un chemin plus lent descendre chez les morts.
J'ai pris, j'ai fait couler dans mes brûlantes veines
Un poison que Médée apporta dans Athènes.
Déjà jusqu'à mon cœur le venin parvenu
Dans ce cœur expirant jette un froid inconnu;
Déjà je ne vois plus qu'à travers un nuage
Et le ciel et l'époux que ma présence outrage;
Et la mort, à mes yeux dérobant la clarté,
Rend au jour, qu'ils souillaient, toute sa pureté.

PANOPE

Elle expire, Seigneur!

THÉSÉE

D'une action si noire
Que ne peut avec elle expirer la mémoire!
Allons, de mon erreur, hélas! trop éclaircis,
Mêler nos pleurs au sang de mon malheureux fils.
Allons de ce cher fils embrasser ce qui reste,
Expier la fureur d'un vœu que je déteste.
Rendons-lui les honneurs qu'il a trop mérités;
Et pour mieux apaiser ses mânes irrités,
Que malgré les complots d'une injuste famille,
Son amante aujourd'hui me tienne lieu de fille.

To accuse him first. For that she soon
Punished herself, and, seeking to escape
My wrath, she sought and found beneath the waves
A far too gentle execution.
By now the sword would have cut short my life,
But that would have left virtue crying out
For justice. I resolved to tell you first
All my remorse, and by a slower path
Descend to death. Wait. I have taken
And through all my burning veins now runs
A poison brought to Athens by Medea.
Already has the venom reached my heart;
This dying heart is filled with—icy cold!
Already only through a mist I see
The Heavens and the husband unto whom
My presence is an outrage. Death removes
The light from eyes which have defiled it, so—
Restores to daylight all its purity.

PANOPE

She's dead, my Lord!

THESEUS
                    I wish the memory
Of her black deed could perish so with her.
Come, all of us who understand at last
Too well my fatal error, let us go,
And with the blood of my unhappy son
Mingle our tears. Let us of my dear son
Embrace the poor remains, and expiate
In deep repentance my detested prayer.
Let him be honoured as he well deserves.
And to appease his so offended ghost—
Whatever were her brothers' crimes, I say
Aricia is my daughter from today.

169

NOTES

NOTES

Preface

Euripides: (480–406 B.C.) was one of the three great Greek dramatists. The play from which the story of *Phèdre* was taken is called *Hippolytus* in Greek.

a little different: Racine's is very different from that of Euripides.

Aristotle: (384–322 B.C.) one of the greatest of Greek philosophers. The reference here is to his treatise on poetry and the drama (the Poetics) which was considered authoritative in Racine's day.

Seneca: (4 B.C.–A.D. 65) a Roman philosopher and dramatist whose plays were admired in Racine's day.

vim corpus tulit: (her) body sustained violence.

Virgil: his version of this story is in the Seventh Book of the *Æneid*.

Æsculapius: the God of medicine.

Plutarch: (about A.D. 46–120) a Greek historian, much delved into by Shakespeare, and everyone else.

Proserpina: also called Persephone; queen of the Underworld and wife of Pluto.

Epirus: a district on the west of the Peloponnesus.

Acheron: a river of Epirus which was supposed to disappear into the underworld.

Socrates: (about 469–399 B.C.) the greatest Greek philosopher, whose conversations were written down by Plato and have never stopped working.

many persons: refers to the Jansenists. Read *God and Mammon* by François Mauriac.

to instruct as to entertain: the same problem exactly as we have today.

The part of Phèdre was played in the original production by
Mlle La Champmêslé.

The Play

Trozene: a city of Peloponnesus, half-way down the coast on the
right.

Hippolytus: son of Theseus and Antiope, the Amazon. When he
spurned the love of his stepmother Phaedra, she slandered him
to her husband Theseus. He was killed and she committed
suicide. A later legend describes him as raised from the dead by
Æsculapius, and worshipped at the sacred grove of Diana at
Aricia in Latium.

Theseus: son of the King of Athens, Ægeus, and, according to
another story, of Poseidon or Neptune, who was, anyway in
Racine's version of the tale, his tutelary god who kept his
promise to grant Theseus' first prayer. Theseus refrained from
using this magic prayer until he came home from a long absence
and found Hippolytus, his son by his first marriage, accused of
having made love to his wife Phaedra. Unfortunately, he then
used it, and Hippolytus, though innocent, was destroyed.

The seas on either side of Corinth: the Ionian and the Ægean
seas.

Elis: a district in the north-west of the Peloponnesus (now
Morea).

Toenarus: the precipitous tip of the middle finger of the claw of
the Greek mainland (now Cape Matapan).

That sea which saw the fall of Icarus: the sea surrounding the
island of Icaria on which the body of Icarus was washed ashore.
Icarus was the son of Daedalus the great inventor and engineer,
who, among other things, constructed the Labyrinth at Knossos
in Crete, at the heart of which lived the Minotaur (q.v.). Icarus
and Daedalus escaped from Crete on wings attached to their
shoulders by wax. But Icarus flew too near the sun, the wax
melted, and he fell into that sea and was drowned.

Theramenes in these four lines is describing what would have
been a tremendous journey. Up from Trozene to Corinth; then

a search along the two coasts on either side of that narrow isthmus; then over to Elis in the extreme north-west; then down to the promontory of Toenarus, and then far out into the Ægean Sea among all those islands. He could hardly have managed it if he had started out before Theseus had been missed! But I suppose the audiences in Racine's time had about as hazy a view of geography as ours now, or this passage might have got a laugh.

Phaedra: daughter of Minos, King of Crete, and of his wife Pasiphaë; younger sister of Ariadne, wife of Theseus, and mother of Acamas and Demophoon.

Minos: King of Crete, son of Zeus and Europa. Poseidon, in answer to his prayer that he should send him a bull for sacrifice, caused a wonderfully beautiful white bull to rise from the sea. Minos wanted to keep it for his herd, so he sacrificed another one, but was punished by Poseidon, or Venus, who made his wife Pasiphaë fall in love with the bull. This penchant was in the family anyway as Zeus had assumed the shape of a bull in order to abduct Europa. In Homer, Odysseus sees Minos in Hades, with a golden sceptre in his hand, judging the shades.

Pasiphaë: daughter of Helios and Perseis, sister of Circe, wife of Minos, and Mother of the Minotaur, Ariadne, and Phaedra. I have never been able to find out in what order, but suppose the Minotaur to have been the youngest, which would account for the eagerness of Ariadne and Phaedra to escape from Crete, and for their subsequent neuroses.

Aricia: see Hippolytus and Preface.

Pallas: son of Pandion who robbed his brother Ægeus of the dominion of Athens, but who was, together with his fifty gigantic sons, killed by the young Theseus.

Venus: Latin goddess of love, identified with Greek goddess Aphrodite. She outshines all the goddesses in grace and loveliness, and presides over love in all its forms. Still does.

Hercules: (Greek Heracles: renowned through Hera) the oldest and most illustrious of the heroes of Greek mythology. Son of Zeus and Alcmene the wife of Amphitryon (whose shape Zeus assumed while Amphitryon was away at a war). He is also called Alcides from alke=strength. He was renowned for twelve labours each requiring superhuman strength, guile and luck. He was also renowned for his numerous love affairs. Theseus took over the monopoly of heroic exploits and love affairs where he left off.

Procrustes: the stretcher: a monster living at Eleusis in Attica. He used to waylay travellers and offer them a bed for the night. If they were too long for it he chopped off the end or ends that protruded; and if too short, he stretched them to fit.

Cercyon: another traveller's terror. He forced people to wrestle with him, and always won, until he met Theseus.

Epidaurus' giant: Periphetes, another road hazard, who killed passers-by with an iron club.

Scirron: a robber, who compelled travellers to wash his feet, in order to be in a position to kick them over a cliff into the sea where they were devoured by an immense tortoise.

Sinnis: he tore travellers to pieces by bending down pine-trees and suddenly letting them go.

Minotaur: the bull of Minos; son of Pasiphaë and the bull sent by Poseidon. He was concealed at the heart of the impenetrable Labyrinth at Knossos, and fed on criminals and also the seven youths and seven maidens exacted as tribute from Athens. Theseus, with the help of Ariadne, killed him and escaped.

Helen: divinely beautiful daughter of Zeus and Leda, of whom there are many legends, one of which represents her as carried off while still a virgin by Theseus, after which she was rescued by her brothers and brought back to Sparta where she was wooed by innumerable suitors of whom she chose Menelaus. She was, during one of his absences, carried off to Troy by Paris and so—as we all know—launched the Trojan War.

Peribœa: one of the girls abandoned by Theseus. She subsequently married Telamon, King of Salamis.

Ariadne: daughter of Minos and Pasiphaë; elder sister of Phaedra. She fell in love with Theseus when he came to Crete as one of the seven youths and seven maidens due to be devoured by the Minotaur. She gave him an unwinding thread by which he might find his way back out of the Labyrinth, which no one had managed to do before; eloped with him and was deserted by him on the island of Naxos. Waking up alone, she was raised up by Dionysus who set her bridal gift, a crown, among the stars. Read *Ariadne on Naxos* by Cecil Day Lewis.

Antiope: sister of Hippolyta queen of the Amazons, who fell as a prize of war to Theseus, or, according to another story, was carried off by him and his friend, Pirithoüs. Her son by Theseus was Hippolytus.

the art that Neptune taught: literally *invented*, horse-riding.

Pirithoüs: Prince of the Lapithae and friend of Theseus. There was a celebrated battle between the Lapithae and the Centaurs who went too far in a drunken brawl at a wedding. Since Theseus rescued the bride, Pirithoüs helped him in the abduction of Helen. Later, Theseus accompanied Pirithoüs into the Underworld in order to carry off Persephone. Pirithoüs came to a bad end and Theseus got back.

Pittheus: King of Trozene, father of Æthra, mother of Theseus. He brought up both Theseus and Hippolytus.

Cocytus: River of cries, a branch of the Styx, one of the rivers of Hades.

Erectheus: mythical King of Athens. According to Homer, he was the son of Earth by Hephaestus and brought up by Athene. Ancestor of Theseus and Pallas.

Ægeus: son of Pandion and Pelia. With the help of his brothers he seized the sole sovereignty of Attica from the sons of his uncle Metion, who had driven out his father. He was dethroned by his brother Pallas, but was rescued and restored by his son Theseus. Having killed Androgeos, son of Minos, he was conquered by Minos and forced to send seven youths and seven maidens to Crete every nine years to be eaten by the Minotaur. When Theseus set out to free his country from this tribute, he promised to hoist a white sail if he should return safely, but forgot, and Ægeus, seeing the black sail returning, gave up hope and toppled off a cliff into the sea which has been named after him.

Noble and blazing author of a race: Pasiphaë, mother of Phaedra, was a daughter of Apollo the Sun god (Helios).

glorious dust: chariot racing was an aristocratic sport.

charm or poison: here used to mean magic potion.

Scythian: the Amazons were said to originate from Scythia, the reputed home of barbarian hordes around the Black Sea.

Oh fatal anger, fatal hate of Venus: the goddess of love caused Pasiphaë to fall in love with the bull, Ariadne to love and be left by Theseus—in fact all the usual disasters.

in their entrails: divination was practised from observation of the entrails of sacrificed animals.

bringing up the sons: this is literally *cultivate the fruits of this fatal marriage*: Acamas and Demophoon.

Pallantides: sons of Pallas (q.v.).

Minerva's citadel: Athens. Minerva, whose Greek name is Athene, built the walls of Athens.

What charm: again used in the sense of magic.

Last offspring of a King: see Erectheus, Pallas and Ægeus.

vainly a mutineer against his joy: this is rather free for what is literally *a yoke that pleases him*, which really cannot be spoken in English.

Always from a safe shore to view their storms: probably a recollection of *Lucretius*, Bk. II, lines 1-2:

> Suave mari magno, turbantibus aequora ventis,
> E terra magnum alterius spectare laborem.

not as the Shades know him: literally: *not as the underworlds have seen him*. The Shades were the ghosts of the dead inhabiting Hades. They were conceived as incorporeal images of their former selves following instinctively their favourite pursuit in life: Orion still a hunter, Minos sitting in judgment as when alive. The King of the Dead was Pluto, and his bride was Proserpina (see Theseus and Pirithoüs).

Monster whom Heaven's bolts have spared too long: Jupiter (Zeus) was thought to smite offending mortals with thunderbolts.

Neptune: God of the Sea, identified with Poseidon, worshipped as God of the Sea and of equestrian accomplishments.

and ... incestuous: we have no noun in English for an incestuous person. Racine here uses three nouns—a *murderer*, a *traitor* and an *incestor*! Well, we cannot, but if the actor fills the pause with additional horror—the adjective sounds all right.

Pillars of Alcides: the rocks on each side of the Straits of Gibraltar were called the Pillars of Hercules.

That dark river: the Styx, one of the rivers in Hades. An oath made upon that name was binding even upon Gods themselves. The other rivers in Hades were Acheron (woe), Cocytus (cries) a branch of the Styx, Phlegethon and Pyriphlegethon (rivers of fire). These two join the waters of Acheron. There is another river Lethe (oblivion) where the souls of the dead drink forgetfulness of their earthly existence. Charon ferried the souls across Acheron into the realms of shadows.

a cruel God: refers to Venus.

Argos and Sparta: two of the most famous cities of ancient Greece.

Ceremonial torches: on the evening of a Greek wedding the bride and bridegroom were conducted to their new home by friends carrying torches with which the first fire was kindled in the house.

Olympus: a mountain in Thessaly, nearly 10,000 feet high. On the topmost peak, which disappeared above the clouds, was supposed to be the abode of the Gods, where there was never wind nor rain but only cloudless splendour.

Diana: Goddess of the Moon, of the open air; of open country with its mountains, streams and brooks, and of the chase, and of childbirth.

Juno: Queen of Heaven, wife of Jupiter. As Goddess of marriage she was invoked at weddings under many names.

Medea: skilled in witchcraft, did several famous poisonings: her adventures with Jason and Ægeus are too long and too well known to tell again here.

Inversions: It is often necessary, for the sake of the rhythm in a line of blank verse, to put an adjective after a noun or to reverse the order in which we would now use words in ordinary speech. This was pointed out to me by Stephen Joseph (see Foreword) as a defect in this translation. I have removed as many as I can, e.g. *When have I ever yet betrayed your faith?* is just as clear and more straightforward than: *When have I ever yet your faith betrayed?* Wherever it is not possible to avoid an inversion I suggest that, if the actor uses the adjective with an emphasis implying that it is an *addition* to his original phrase, e.g. *You go to meet your end—inevitable!* it will not sound stilted. Here and there I have used inversions, deliberately, e.g. Œnone says: *and well you know*. Which is more appropriate to the speech of a servant than: *and you know well*. And *a hatred fierce* sounds fine if she speaks it as if seeking the adjective.

We always have to do by intonation in English what is done by grammar in French.

P.S. It is not practical to ask friends' advice about translation, as everyone has ideas. But I must express my sincere thanks to Frank Beecroft, who is Head of Modern Languages at Bristol Grammar School and who shares my passion for Racine; and to Stephen Joseph who started the whole thing and suggested many improvements.

M.R.

FOR THE BEST IN PAPERBACKS, LOOK FOR THE

In every corner of the world, on every subject under the sun, Penguin represents quality and variety—the very best in publishing today.

For complete information about books available from Penguin—including Pelicans, Puffins, Peregrines, and Penguin Classics—and how to order them, write to us at the appropriate address below. Please note that for copyright reasons the selection of books varies from country to country.

In the United Kingdom: For a complete list of books available from Penguin in the U.K., please write to *Dept E.P., Penguin Books Ltd, Harmondsworth, Middlesex, UB7 0DA.*

In the United States: For a complete list of books available from Penguin in the U.S., please write to *Consumer Sales, Penguin USA, P.O. Box 999— Dept. 17109, Bergenfield, New Jersey 07621-0120.* VISA and MasterCard holders call 1-800-253-6476 to order all Penguin titles.

In Canada: For a complete list of books available from Penguin in Canada, please write to *Penguin Books Canada Ltd, 10 Alcorn Avenue, Suite 300, Toronto, Ontario, Canada M4V 3B2.*

In Australia: For a complete list of books available from Penguin in Australia, please write to the *Marketing Department, Penguin Books Ltd, P.O. Box 257, Ringwood, Victoria 3134.*

In New Zealand: For a complete list of books available from Penguin in New Zealand, please write to the *Marketing Department, Penguin Books (NZ) Ltd, Private Bag, Takapuna, Auckland 9.*

In India: For a complete list of books available from Penguin, please write to *Penguin Overseas Ltd, 706 Eros Apartments, 56 Nehru Place, New Delhi, 110019.*

In Holland: For a complete list of books available from Penguin in Holland, please write to *Penguin Books Nederland B.V., Postbus 195, NL-1380AD Weesp, Netherlands.*

In Germany: For a complete list of books available from Penguin, please write to *Penguin Books Ltd, Friedrichstrasse 10-12, D-6000 Frankfurt Main 1, Federal Republic of Germany.*

In Spain: For a complete list of books available from Penguin in Spain, please write to *Longman, Penguin España, Calle San Nicolas 15, E-28013 Madrid, Spain.*

In Japan: For a complete list of books available from Penguin in Japan, please write to *Longman Penguin Japan Co Ltd, Yamaguchi Building, 2-12-9 Kanda Jimbocho, Chiyoda-Ku, Tokyo 101, Japan.*

FOR THE BEST IN CLASSICS, LOOK FOR THE

☐ HARD TIMES

Charles Dickens

A powerful portrait of a Lancashire mill town in the 1840s, *Hard Times* stigmatized the prevalent philosophy of Utilitarianism which allowed human beings to be enslaved to machines and reduced to numbers.

328 pages   ISBN: 0-14-043042-3

☐ GREAT EXPECTATIONS

Charles Dickens

In the story of the orphan Pip and the mysterious fortune which falls into his lap, Dickens developed a theme that would preoccupy him towards the end of his life — How do men know who they are?

512 pages   ISBN: 0-14-043003-2

☐ WALDEN & CIVIL DISOBEDIENCE

Henry David Thoreau

"If a man does not keep pace with his companions, perhaps it is because he hears a different drummer." Conveying Thoreau's wonder at the commonplace and his yearning for spiritual truth and self-reliance, *Walden* is both a naturalist's and a Transcendentalist's account of the beauty of solitude.

432 pages   ISBN: 0-14-039044-8

☐ JANE EYRE

Charlotte Brontë

One of the most widely read of all English novels, *Jane Eyre* depicts the refusal of a spirited and intelligent woman to accept her appointed place in society with unusual frankness and with a passionate sense of the dignity and needs of women.

490 pages   ISBN: 0-14-043011-3

You can find all these books at your local bookstore, or use this handy coupon for ordering:

Penguin Books By Mail
Dept. BA Box 999
Bergenfield, NJ 07621-0999

Please send me the above title(s). I am enclosing _____
(please add sales tax if appropriate and $1.50 to cover postage and handling). Send check or money order—no CODs. Please allow four weeks for shipping. We cannot ship to post office boxes or addresses outside the USA. *Prices subject to change without notice.*

Ms./Mrs./Mr. _____

Address _____

City/State _____ Zip _____

FOR THE BEST IN CLASSICS, LOOK FOR THE

☐ WUTHERING HEIGHTS

Emily Brontë

An intensely original work, this story of the passionate love between Cathy and Heathcliff is recorded with such truth, imagination, and emotional intensity that it acquires the depth and simplicity of ancient tragedy.

372 pages   ISBN: 0-14-043001-6

☐ UTOPIA

Thomas More

Utopia revolutionized Plato's classical blueprint of the perfect republic, and can be seen as the source of Anabaptism, Mormonism, and even Communism. Witty, immediate, vital, prescient, it is the work of a man who drank deep of the finest spirit of his age.

154 pages   ISBN: 0-14-044165-4

☐ THE SCARLET LETTER

Nathaniel Hawthorne

Publicly disgraced and ostracized by the harsh Puritan community of seven-teenth-century Boston, Hester Prynne draws on her inner strength to emerge as the first true heroine of American fiction.

284 pages   ISBN: 0-14-039019-7

☐ WINESBURG, OHIO

Sherwood Anderson

Introduced as "The Tales and the Persons," this timeless cycle of short stories lays bare the lives of the friendly but solitary people of small town America at the turn of the century.

248 pages   ISBN: 0-14-039059-6

☐ CANDIDE

Voltaire

One of the glories of eighteenth-century satire, *Candide* was the most brilliant challenge to the prevailing thought that held "all is for the best in the best of all possible worlds."

144 pages   ISBN: 0-14-044004-6

☐ PRIDE AND PREJUDICE

Jane Austen

While Napoleon transformed Europe, Jane Austen wrote a novel in which a man changes his manners and a young lady her mind. In Austen's world of delicious social comedy, the truly civilized being maintains a proper balance between rea-son and energy.

400 pages   ISBN: 0-14-043072-5

FOR THE BEST IN CLASSICS, LOOK FOR THE

☐ **THE ODYSSEY**

Homer

E. V. Rieu's best-selling prose translation captures both the delicacy and drama of the hero Odysseus's journey and allows the freshness and excitement of Homer's well-knit plot to delight us as much as it did the ancient Greeks.

368 pages   ISBN: 0-14-044001-1

☐ **THE PRINCE**

Niccolo Machiavelli

This treatise on statecraft — in which the author uncompromisingly proposes what most governments do but none profess to do — holds such power to shock that at one time Machiavelli was identified with Satan himself.

154 pages   ISBN: 0-14-044107-7

☐ **HEART OF DARKNESS**

Joseph Conrad

Written in the last year of the nineteenth century, *Heart of Darkness* represents in many ways the first twentieth-century novel. Conrad's story of Marlow's search for Mr. Kurtz provides an extraordinary exploration of human savagery and despair.

122 pages   ISBN: 0-14-043168-3

☐ **THE CANTERBURY TALES**

Geoffrey Chaucer

Told by a motley crowd of pilgrims journeying from Southwark to Canterbury, these tales — bawdy, pious, erudite, tragic, comic — reveal a picture of four-teenth-century England which is as robust as it is representative.

526 pages   ISBN: 0-14-044022-4

You can find all these books at your local bookstore, or use this handy coupon for ordering:

Penguin Books By Mail
Dept. BA Box 999
Bergenfield, NJ 07621-0999

Please send me the above title(s). I am enclosing _____
(please add sales tax if appropriate and $1.50 to cover postage and handling). Send check or money order—no CODs. Please allow four weeks for shipping. We cannot ship to post office boxes or addresses outside the USA. *Prices subject to change without notice.*

Ms./Mrs./Mr. _____

Address _____

City/State _____ Zip _____

FOR THE BEST IN CLASSICS, LOOK FOR THE

☐ THE RED BADGE OF COURAGE

Stephen Crane

Certainly one of the greatest novels written about the heat of battle, Crane's story ultimately concerns the battle waged in young Henry Fleming's mind as he reacts to "reality," confronts duty and fear, and comes to terms with himself and the world.

222 pages   ISBN: 0-14-039021-9

☐ McTEAGUE

Frank Norris

This searing portrait of the downfall of a slow-witted dentist and his avaricious wife is a novel of compelling narrative force and a powerful and shocking example of early American realism.

442 pages   ISBN: 0-14-039017-0

☐ SELECTED ESSAYS

Ralph Waldo Emerson

With these essays calling for harmony with nature and reliance on individual integrity, Emerson unburdened his young country of Europe's traditional sense of history and showed Americans how to be creators of their own circumstances.

416 pages   ISBN: 0-14-039013-8

☐ SISTER CARRIE

Theodore Dreiser

This unsparing story of a country girl's rise to riches as the mistress of a wealthy man is a pioneering work of naturalism, especially so in this unexpurgated edition which follows Dreiser's original manuscript.

500 pages   ISBN: 0-14-039002-2

☐ UNCLE TOM'S CABIN

Harriet Beecher Stowe

A powerful indictment of slavery that brought the abolitionists' message to the White House and beyond, *Uncle Tom's Cabin* was hailed by Tolstoy as "one of the greatest productions of the human mind."

630 pages   ISBN: 0-14-039003-0

☐ THE ADVENTURES OF HUCKLEBERRY FINN

Mark Twain

"All modern American literature comes from one book by Mark Twain called *Huckleberry Finn*," wrote Ernest Hemingway. An incomparable adventure story and a classic of American humor, no book has a better claim to the title of The Great American Novel.

336 pages   ISBN: 0-14-039046-4

☐ **"MASTER HAROLD" . . . AND THE BOYS**
  Athol Fugard

A stunning exploration of apartheid and racism, *"Master Harold" . . . and the boys* "is beyond beauty." (Frank Rich, *The New York Times*)
                    60 pages   ISBN: 0-14-048187-7

☐ **CONTEMPORARY SCENES FOR STUDENT ACTORS**
  Edited by Michael Schulman and Eva Mekler

Containing more than 80 scenes by major modern playwrights, *Contemporary Scenes for Student Actors* includes dialogues for two men, two women, and one man and one woman.
                    438 pages   ISBN: 0-14-048153-2

FOR THE BEST DRAMA, LOOK FOR THE

☐ **THE CRUCIBLE**
Arthur Miller

Arthur Miller's classic dramatization of the Salem witch hunt, *The Crucible* is a chilling tale of mass hysteria, fear, and the power of suggestion.

152 pages   ISBN: 0-14-048138-9

☐ **PYGMALION**
Bernard Shaw

Shaw's portrayal of a Cockney flower girl's metamorphosis into a lady is not only a delightful fantasy but also an intriguing commentary on social class, money, spiritual freedom, and women's independence.

152 pages   ISBN: 0-14-045022-X

☐ **EQUUS**
Peter Shaffer

A deranged youth blinds six horses with a spike. A psychiatrist tries to help him. But what is help? *Equus* is a brilliant examination of the decay of modern man.

112 pages   ISBN: 0-14-048185-0

☐ **THE ACTOR'S BOOK OF CONTEMPORARY STAGE MONOLOGUES**
Edited by Nina Shengold

This unique anthology provides a wealth of materials for actors and acting students, and a wonderful overview of the best of recent plays for anyone interested in the theater.

356 pages   ISBN: 0-14-009649-3